FROM INFORMATION LITERACY TO SOCIAL EPISTEMOLOGY

AF795406

CHANDOS
INFORMATION PROFESSIONAL SERIES

Series Editor: Ruth Rikowski
(email: Rikowskigr@aol.com)

Chandos' new series of books is aimed at the busy information professional. They have been specially commissioned to provide the reader with an authoritative view of current thinking. They are designed to provide easy-to-read and (most importantly) practical coverage of topics that are of interest to librarians and other information professionals. If you would like a full listing of current and forthcoming titles, please visit www.chandospublishing.com.

New authors: we are always pleased to receive ideas for new titles; if you would like to write a book for Chandos, please contact Dr Glyn Jones on g.jones.2@elsevier.com or telephone +44 (0) 1865 843000.

FROM INFORMATION LITERACY TO SOCIAL EPISTEMOLOGY

Insights from Psychology

ANTHONY ANDERSON
BILL JOHNSTON

ELSEVIER

AMSTERDAM • BOSTON • HEIDELBERG • LONDON
NEW YORK • OXFORD • PARIS • SAN DIEGO
SAN FRANCISCO • SINGAPORE • SYDNEY • TOKYO
Chandos Publishing is an imprint of Elsevier

CP
CHANDOS
PUBLISHING

Chandos Publishing is an imprint of Elsevier
50 Hampshire Street, 5th Floor, Cambridge, MA 02139, USA
The Boulevard, Langford Lane, Kidlington, OX5 1GB, UK

Copyright © 2016 A. Anderson and B. Johnston. Published by Elsevier Ltd.
All rights reserved.

No part of this publication may be reproduced or transmitted in any form or by any means, electronic or mechanical, including photocopying, recording, or any information storage and retrieval system, without permission in writing from the publisher. Details on how to seek permission, further information about the Publisher's permissions policies and our arrangements with organizations such as the Copyright Clearance Center and the Copyright Licensing Agency, can be found at our website: www.elsevier.com/permissions.

This book and the individual contributions contained in it are protected under copyright by the Publisher (other than as may be noted herein).

Notices
Knowledge and best practice in this field are constantly changing. As new research and experience broaden our understanding, changes in research methods, professional practices, or medical treatment may become necessary.

Practitioners and researchers must always rely on their own experience and knowledge in evaluating and using any information, methods, compounds, or experiments described herein. In using such information or methods they should be mindful of their own safety and the safety of others, including parties for whom they have a professional responsibility.

To the fullest extent of the law, neither the Publisher nor the authors, contributors, or editors, assume any liability for any injury and/or damage to persons or property as a matter of products liability, negligence or otherwise, or from any use or operation of any methods, products, instructions, or ideas contained in the material herein.

British Library Cataloguing-in-Publication Data
A catalogue record for this book is available from the British Library

Library of Congress Cataloging-in-Publication Data
A catalog record for this book is available from the Library of Congress

ISBN: 978-0-08-100545-3 (print)
ISBN: 978-0-08-100548-4 (online)

For information on all Chandos Publishing publications
visit our website at https://www.elsevier.com/

Working together to grow libraries in developing countries

www.elsevier.com • www.bookaid.org

Publisher: Glyn Jones
Acquisition Editor: Glyn Jones
Editorial Project Manager: Harriet Clayton
Production Project Manager: Debasish Ghosh
Designer: Victoria Pearson Esser

CONTENTS

Preface *ix*

Section A Introduction and Background **1**

1. Introduction **3**
- 1.1 The Information Culture: Information Literacy and Digital Participation 3
- 1.2 Information Literacy – A Key Enabler of Participation? 8
- 1.3 Psychology and Psychological Insights – Cognition, Metacognition and Critical Thinking 11
- 1.4 Conclusion and Structure of the Book 13

2. Information Literacy in Adult Returner Students: The Pre-Entry Class Case Study **19**
- 2.1 The Background Context 19
- 2.2 The Study Itself 22
- 2.3 Summary 29
- 2.4 Corroborative Studies 29
- 2.5 Conclusions 31

Section B Psychological Insights **35**

3. Critical Thinking and Information Literacy **37**
- 3.1 Critical Thinking 37
- 3.2 The Quality of Argumentative Reasoning 41
- 3.3 Pedagogy and Critical Thinking: Attempts to Improve the Quality of Critical Thinking via Teaching Interventions 47
- 3.4 Conclusions 52

4. Epistemological Thinking, Metacognition and Their Relation to Critical Thinking and Information Literacy **53**
- 4.1 Introduction 53
- 4.2 The Development of Epistemological Thinking 54
- 4.3 Metacognition 60
- 4.4 Epistemic Metacognition 65
- 4.5 Conclusions 66

5. Student Learning and Information Literacy **67**
5.1 Introduction 67
5.2 Constructivism 67
5.3 Critique of Constructivism 73
5.4 Study Skills 74
5.5 Conclusion: Implications for Information Literacy Instruction 75

Section C Contributions from the Library and Information Sector **81**

6. Curriculum Development and the New Curriculum for Information Literacy **83**
6.1 Introduction 83
6.2 Transformational Learning 85
6.3 Curriculum Inquiry and Practice: Tools for Transformation 92
6.4 Curriculum Development 93
6.5 Information Literacy and Curriculum Development 95
6.6 New Curriculum for Information Literacy: A Helicopter View for Busy Educationalists 96
6.7 Conclusions 101

7. The ACRL (2000) Standards and the ACRL (2015) Revised Framework **103**
7.1 Introduction 103
7.2 Pedagogical Changes 106
7.3 Threshold Concepts Critique 107
7.4 Pedagogical Implications 112
7.5 Definition of Information Literacy in the ACRL Framework 113
7.6 Conclusions 114

8. UNESCO Contributions to Information Literacy **115**
8.1 Introduction: Education, Information, Human Rights and Social Justice 115
8.2 UNESCO Contribution 1: Proclamations 117
8.3 UNESCO Contribution 2: Information Literacy Primer (Woody Horton) 118
8.4 UNESCO Contribution 3: Media and Information Literacy (MIL) 121
8.5 UNESCO Contribution 4: Knowledge Societies (2015) Final Study 124
8.6 Conclusion 127

Section D Social Epistemology **129**

9. Information Literacy and Social Epistemology **131**

9.1 Introduction 131
9.2 Social Epistemology 132
9.3 Pedagogy for Social Epistemology 145
9.4 Conclusions 151

References *153*
Index *161*

PREFACE

This book combines current academic, professional and policy perspectives on information literacy (IL) with insights from cognitive psychology. Our view of information literacy is twofold, encompassing both the micro-experiences of individuals and small groups seeking information, for example students, and the macro-organization of information to meet wider societal needs. Our view of psychology is framed by a judicious selection of the most relevant concepts from cognitive psychology, for example epistemological thinking, metacognition and critical thinking, which are pertinent to pedagogy and information use.

Our intention is to provide library and information science (LIS) professionals and others, such as LIS lecturers, their students and researchers in the field of information literacy with a new perspective on key questions such as:

- How might educators apply psychological reasoning to the design of educational initiatives to improve information literacy?
- How can information literacy be studied and enhanced as an aspect of information activity in the general population?
- How can information literacy be understood and developed more widely as a lifelong learning experience for larger numbers of people?
- What is the nature of critical thinking and how does information literacy relate to critical thinking in education, lifelong learning and social life?

In addition we hope to provide lecturers in other disciplines with an enhanced appreciation of information literacy, which they can adapt to their teaching, and incorporate in their curriculum development activities. We would also hope that readers will be able to apply our ideas to organisational development in their institutions and finally we aim to contribute to a better understanding of the role of information in society.

Our starting point is the often-cited UNESCO proposal (2003, 2005, 2006) that information literacy is a human right and is essential to lifelong learning. The implication of this perspective is that there is a wide range of behaviours and activities distributed across the population, which share the essential features of IL as described in professional and research-based definitions, statements of standards such as that by ACRL, and the academic and professional literature. However, it is clear from the UNESCO view, that the incidence, proportions and interactions of such behaviour and activity are unevenly distributed across even educated populations and are therefore in need of significant teaching and learning interventions to match UNESCO's aspirations. This is a disturbing state of affairs in a time when the Internet, digital technologies and social media are enhancing the visibility of information as a powerful socioeconomic and political resource.

We therefore explore why, despite such high-level policy support and the significant amount of work carried out by LIS professionals and others, IL remains relatively unknown in public and educational policy outside the interests of a relatively specific stakeholder group. Candidate explanations for the cause of this situation include: overemphasis on digital technologies; assumptions about the capacity of younger and older people to manage technology; lack of development of information literacy in formal education; and the absence of a powerful lobby for information literacy in policymaking. Equally, we propose some remedies for this situation by proposing a new way of comprehending information literacy based in psychological insights. For example, we review psychological theorising on the nature of student learning and based on that we advocate the use of structured peer interaction as a pedagogical method for inculcating information-literacy-related concepts and skills. Discussion of potential educational strategies predominates in the book; however, we also use the concept of social epistemology to develop our discussion of the wider social and cultural dimensions of information literacy.

The impetus for the book arose from the authors' mutual interests in the nature of information literacy in the wider population, both within and outside the familiar contexts of education and the workplace. We were equally interested in questions of how information and information literacy relate to critical thinking in education and the workplace, but also in social life generally. The broad context for our interest is the development in Internet technologies often characterised by terms like the 'Digital Age', leading to questions of digital participation, digital divides, and the role of thinking in the information society. In short – to what extent is the 'Digital Age' engendering changes in learning directed towards the better use of information, and in addition encouraging or even requiring improvements in critical thinking?

Our interests are grounded in our backgrounds in academic research and teaching in psychology, pedagogy and information literacy in higher education. Our initial strategy for pursuing broad questions about the quality of information literacy within the general population was to identify and research a representative group of adults who were in the process of returning to higher education via a course of study designed to meet that purpose and support transitions to formal academic study. We argue that the sample involved might represent a condensed example of the major relations between adult learning and information literacy in the digital age. Our findings convinced us that whilst information literacy is a key aspect of such learning journeys, and a significant feature of life within the adult population, it is both undervalued in teaching and also insufficient in itself to achieve better learning.

The details of our research are presented in this book (see Chapter 2) as a case study drawing together our larger concerns in a practical and manageable form. That case study was published (Anderson, Johnson, and MacDonald, 2013) as '*Information literacy in adult returners to higher education: Student experiences in a university pre-entry course in a UK university*' which was judged to be a top-20 paper of 2013 by the ACRL Roundtable Top Twenty Committee.

Conducting the research and writing the journal paper caused us to look more closely at related concepts from psychology, and in particular, the notions of metacognition/metastrategy and epistemology in relation to information literacy. We also looked more closely at pedagogical concepts, particularly patterns of learning and teaching, and transformational learning as major aspects of the nature of courses and curriculum development for adults. Each of these psychological and pedagogical constructs is described in chapters of this book, in order to provide non-specialist readers with a guide to the research literature. Each of these areas of research is reviewed and summarised, and its implications for information literacy, pedagogy and the wider information society is articulated as far as is possible.

LIS professionals and many educators have been active for some decades in pursuing an optimal form of information literacy in education, the workplace and public library practice. All of these efforts are valuable and have influenced our thinking, to the extent that we position ourselves as 'critical friends' to the LIS and education communities. The ACRL Top Twenty Committee citation noted that:

> *[o]f note are the authors' backgrounds; none is a librarian. The research team is comprised of a curriculum developer, a lecturer in psychology, and a practitioner who runs the pre-entry course. Their study, which echoes previous calls for librarian participation in curriculum design, might help convey this call to a broader audience.*

Consequently we have applied our insights into adult learning and the information society to several current developments in the LIS field: Secker and Coonan's Curriculum for IL (2013; see Chapter 6); the ACRL Standards which are currently in process of revision (ACRL, 2000, 2015; see Chapter 7); UNESCO's decision to propose the combined notion of Media and Information Literacy (see Chapter 8).

We are committed to balancing varied audience interests. For example:

- The need for instructional librarians to develop more theoretically sound and pedagogically effective ways of getting students to learn IL concepts/ techniques and then assessing their knowledge and competence.
- The desire from information academics to see a more theoretically informed text on IL.
- The aspiration from IL experts to advocate IL with institutional leaders, in order to build more coherent and better-resourced IL systems for the institution as a whole.
- The aspiration for committed individuals to see IL presented in relation to big social issues of inequality, social justice and human rights.

Our book appears at an exciting time for information literacy scholars and practitioners. The longstanding emphasis on a skills-based account of information literacy is now balanced by a focus on information literacy as information practices situated in a given context. For example, one significant component of information literacy, we will argue throughout this book, is critical thinking and in particular argumentative reasoning. Schwartz, Newman, Gil, and Ilya (2003) compared the theoretical conceptualisation of argumentative reasoning as a skill, as opposed to its conceptualisation as an activity. The skills perspective conceives of argumentative reasoning as a feature of the individual that can be more or less well developed depending on how much training and practice they have had with such skills; the skills are thus seen as 'in' the individual, an enduring if changeable (through education/practice) feature of the person. The activity perspective (some would use the phrase 'situated activity') is slightly more subtle in recognising that individuals interact with situational constraints (for example, task demands, other people) and their performance is therefore inevitably affected by the situation in which they act. The quality of performance is therefore not solely a function of the person's supposed skill level, but of the interaction of the person with the situation. This situated activity perspective is more in line with our own thinking, and in our view the idea of situated information literacy encompasses both the search and the evaluation phases of information literacy activities: there is every reason to believe that search processes are likely to also be context-sensitive. The situated activity view extends beyond the earlier attention paid to using information for learning in educational settings and now includes everyday life situations in workplaces, the marketplace, political decision-making and a variety of other areas. Throughout the book we develop and discuss a four-element model of the generic information literacy system, comprising the elements (1) the person, with their varied and changing characteristics; (2) the information entity (the wide range of information-bearing entities that can be in use within such situations); (3) the context of use (which can vary from formal educational contexts to individual leisure use, for example) and (4) the subject matter or academic discipline (which varies enormously from, eg, science topics through arts topics, to general knowledge and hobby topics, each with its characteristic standards of practice and of evidence). It is our fundamental contention that any information literacy situation has to be seen as an interaction among these four elements.

Clearly a broader appreciation of information literacy is developing, which extends beyond search skills for study purposes and an academically oriented idea of problem-solving and critical thinking. For example, Google, the emblematic information entity and ubiquitous search tool of contemporary society, can be seen as affording not simply information, but an opportunity for users to establish the significance of information in relation to a person's needs in a given context as they intersect with that person's notions of the nature and value of knowledge – in short *their epistemological beliefs*.

The matter of epistemology, both individual and social, is a key theme for information literacy in the coming years and our book will develop the concept from a basis in cognitive psychology applied to learning, pedagogy and social engagement. Our perspective is a shift from a searching perspective to one characterised by much greater attention to construction of knowledge and personal agency in a variety of social contexts. The online world of 21st-century mass media, social media, news, digital commerce and lifelong learning cannot be easily understood without consideration of the epistemological beliefs, actions and ethical standards of online citizens. Greater access to information and greater emphasis on information in our lives, brings with it the challenge of how to establish credibility, reliability and utility. In the public sphere we are also challenged as citizens to negotiate propaganda, misinformation, hoaxes, scams and outright corruption as part of our information practice. *Hence our emphasis on epistemology and in particular the concept of social epistemology*.

These exciting developments in the concept of information literacy are mirrored by equally important developments in the approaches being taken by practitioners, particularly in education. The decision by ACRL in the

USA to move from an approach to instruction based on a listing of Standards (ACRL, 2000) to a new and developing Framework (ACRL, 2015) drawing on the pedagogical research on threshold concepts (see, eg, Meyer and Land, 2003), which originated in the UK, is of major significance. The starting point for ACRL was recognition that pedagogical changes in US higher education teaching practice was changing the learning context of US students and that this change required a response, which would provide librarians with a new basis for their instructional practice. That ACRL incorporated ideas from pedagogical research is a key development, which we will discuss in detail (Chapter 7).

This major move in the USA is mirrored in the UK by Jane Secker and Emma Coonan's work on the New Curriculum for information literacy (Secker and Coonan, 2013). This work represents a significant drawing together of ideas about the nature of information literacy in pedagogical practice and in line with ACRL seeks to provide a wider and more comprehensive approach to embedding information literacy at the level of course design and educational development in higher education institutions.

Both these developments are at a relatively early stage of acceptance, adoption and evaluation in practice so a detailed critique is inappropriate. However several key features are worth noting: neither sets out a simple 'formulae' or 'checklist' of items to be implemented more or less as given; both call out for participation by librarians, lecturers and institutional leaders in creating a new generation of information literacy education; both imply a major renovation in pedagogical practice from the dominant 'one-slot shot' approach to much more complex and integrated forms. Our discussion is aimed, therefore, at contributing to that change process and we have adopted the role of critical friends to our colleagues in the USA, the UK and elsewhere, who are engaged in the work.

As a global community we are faced by major challenges in the areas of climate change, demography, migration, health and ageing populations. We are facing these challenges against a backdrop of growing inequalities in wealth and educational attainment. The demands on freedom of speech, intercultural awareness, political decision-making and our basic ability to make a decent living are substantial. We cannot all be scientific experts in all the fields necessary to understand and influence change. This problem is another that has been thoroughly discussed in the psychology literature, and goes by the name of transfer of learning. A number of studies, starting with the classic work of Gick and Holyoak (1980) have demonstrated that knowledge gained in one context or from solving one problem does not necessarily transfer readily to another problem; see McKeough, Lupart and Marini (2010), for a sample of studies and discussions on this subject. As we will see in Chapter 3, some theorists doubt whether critical thinking transfers across disciplinary contexts (and espouse so-called domain-specific theories of critical thinking). This might well imply that an individual would be capable of critical thinking in a particular disciplinary context that he/she had studied extensively but this critical faculty might not manifest itself in the case of content from other domains of knowledge. This potential lack of transfer from one context to another is just as much a major challenge to information literacy scholars and practitioners as it is to educators in any other discipline. We do not have the space to review the extensive literature on transfer within this book. We do, however, have some straightforward recommendations to make regarding how to encourage transfer of learning. In essence the problem is one of concepts and skills (eg, critical thinking skills) that are learned in one context needing to be seen to be relevant for use, and subsequently being used, in another context. For example, a critical thinking skill that is learned in a formal academic context such as a degree course such as biology might profitably be brought to bear on more everyday matters, such as evaluating politicians' or marketers' claims regarding policies and products. In order to increase the likelihood of such transfer occurring, our suggestion would be that the relevant instruction should include both formal and less formal examples (eg, in the latter case, newspaper or magazine articles reporting on issues relevant to the course content). Such less formal examples provide good opportunities to practice and hone critical thinking skills, which we see as being central to all phases of any information literacy activity.

To summarise, after a broad introduction to the whole area of information literacy in Section A of the book, we spend Section B of the book discussing key aspects of psychology (critical thinking, epistemological thinking and metacognition) that we argue underpin information literacy activities, and in consequence the design of information literacy education should explicitly aim to address these three fundamental psychological aspects. In Section C we review contributions from ACRL, Secker and Coonan (2013) and UNESCO in the light of the psychological material considered in Section B. Finally, in Section D (Chapter 9) we broaden the discussion to advocate conceptualisation of information literacy as a kind of social epistemology. We hope that readers will find the theoretical discussion stimulating, the pedagogical and practical implications intriguing and potentially useful in their practice, and the broader social epistemology thought-provoking.

SECTION A

Introduction and Background

CHAPTER 1

Introduction

The concept of *information culture* is used to describe the social behaviours, economic activities and educational environments of modern societies. The Internet/world wide web and digital technologies are key infrastructure for such societies. The growth of digital and other information resources in addition to traditional sources, and the convergence of ownership and control in global corporations, emphasises the need for people to develop information literacy in order to function as business leaders, managers, professionals, workers, consumers, learners and critical citizens. The *psychological competencies* and *pedagogical strategies* required to inculcate information literacy are described and related to the concept of *social epistemology*.

1.1 THE INFORMATION CULTURE: INFORMATION LITERACY AND DIGITAL PARTICIPATION

Humans engage with information from birth, taking in messages from their immediate environment and communicating their needs to their parents and carers. In the first months of life the 'information' involved is largely biological and emotional, generated by the organism's need for food, care, acknowledgement and emotional comfort. This early experience of biosocial information is fundamental to human survival, subsequent development, socialisation, learning, productivity, organisation and creativity. The idea of an 'information society' may seem a child of the 20th century but from our perspective, humans have been immersed in information for millennia.

To press the image somewhat, humans engage with information much as they engage with oxygen – breathing is a natural aspect of life and so too is the gathering and sharing of information. Whilst in contemporary parlance the concept 'information' is associated with text and graphics, particularly as presented in books and by computer systems, it is worth bearing in mind that the term 'information' has much wider applicability than that. For example, psychologists interested in visual perception have articulated the concept of *affordances*. These are the uses to which a perceived object can be put, and the implied interactions that we can have with objects that are derived from their visible appearance. For example, as we sit in the driver's seat of a car,

Copyright © 2016 A. Anderson and B. Johnston.
Published by Elsevier Ltd.
All rights reserved.
From Information Literacy to Social Epistemology
ISBN 978-0-08-100545-3

the steering wheel visibly affords turning, the indicator switches afford pushing, the volume knob on the sound system affords turning, and the pedals in the driver's footwell afford pushing with one's feet. These perceptions are available to us even if we do not know the functions of these various controls, as for example would be in the case of an adult or a child who has never learnt to drive. Such an individual would know just by looking at a car's controls what kinds of actions can be taken on them, even if he or she did not know what the controls actually did. (The interested reader can find a fuller discussion of affordances and their consequences in Donald Norman's engaging book, *The Psychology of Everyday Things*: Norman, 2013.) The point at stake here is that as humans we are immersed in information coming from the perceived world; this of course includes auditory information (eg, the train driver who monitors the progress of his journey at night in part from the changes in sounds reaching him as the train goes over bridges or through tunnels), perceptible tactile information, and even perceptible temperature variation. (If this last example seems fanciful, we suggest that you consult a professional firefighter on this point; see Lloyd, 2010.)

As humans develop, their information activities grow in scope and sophistication beyond the essentials for survival. This gradual development is supported by parents, peers, teachers, librarians and many others with the aim of preparing individuals to take part in their society, economy, politics and human culture in all its manifestations.

These personal engagements are at the root of human information behaviour, but are easily overlooked as we concentrate on more formal information activities involving the learning and use of cultural tools such as reading, writing, speech and the various information entities linked to these tools. It is therefore easy to forget that human information behaviour is *relational and transactional*, rather than a simple response to external entities containing information such as books, pictures, lessons, lectures, computers and the Internet. Human relationships constitute the various information ecosystems, which can be discerned in societies at given points in their histories, evolving through agricultural, industrial and knowledge-based forms of social production and economic relationships.

1.1.1 The Information Culture

It is a truism that the impact of the Internet has been revolutionary on all aspects of human culture. For example, Deuze (2006) discusses the emergence of a 'digital culture' as part of a shift away from 19th-century print culture to a 21st-century digital culture in which networked computers, multiple-user software and the Internet become the dominant medium for the production, distribution and communication of culture. This is exemplified by such phenomena as the growth of independent online journalism and blogging. The pervasiveness and extraordinary growth in use of these technologies raises for us a large number of fascinating questions concerning people's competence to function in this virtual environment (ie, their information literacy), the psychological issues surrounding the learning of the required competences, and the pedagogical issues concerning how best to inculcate information literacy. It also highlights the inherently social nature of digital participation: when we access the world wide web in search of information, for example, we are accessing materials produced by other people, raising issues about how we judge its provenance, accuracy and trustworthiness. Such epistemological questions are therefore given an inherently social dimension and the development in recent years of a specifically social epistemology is both centrally relevant and extremely helpful. This notion of *social epistemology* is developed throughout this book and discussed most fully in Chapter 9.

Our starting premise therefore is that *digital information* is a key learning, employment, cultural and everyday life resource for all citizens in contemporary culture, which takes visible form in websites, emails, texts, Internet searches, blogposts, social media and many other channels. These relatively new channels complement the rich pattern of information channels such as books, newspapers, personal communications and other social forms, which have sustained cultural participation over the centuries. For citizens to fully benefit from digital participation in 21st-century culture it is essential that they not only have access to a base level of relevant technology, online systems and assistance to get online, but that they also develop sophisticated knowledge and skills in creating, accessing and managing the information processes and content represented in their digital technologies and devices. In effect the 'literacy' of online digital activity is perceived here as the literacy of information, hence the use of the term information literacy rather than the term *digital literacy*.

At present there is much emphasis on *digital* information. However, some critical analysis is needed. For example, we should at this early stage challenge the increasingly artificial distinction between the 'digital' and the 'informational'. These are ceasing to be discrete entities, but instead massively overlap. Crucially, uses of the digital and the informational emerge out of their relationships to human engagements and purposes such as study, decision-making, communication and so on.

A necessary first step before discussing information literacy is to provide a working definition of the concept of 'information'. There is a plethora of definitions of this concept (see Buckland, 1991, for a discussion, for example). However, one useful definition for the purposes of the present discussion is the long-established engineering notion of uncertainty reduction: information reduces our uncertainty. This superficially simple definition usefully highlights some subtle aspects of information. In particular, it makes it clear that information is relational rather than absolute in nature: a given piece of text, for example, may be highly informative to one individual but much less so to another (eg, one who is already familiar with its content). As such, information (uncertainty reduction) is not 'in' the text, but in the relation between the text and the reader. This brings such issues as the prior knowledge of the seeker of information to centre-stage. It also highlights the information seeker/user as an active participant rather than a passive recipient, given that he/she has the task of assessing the significance *for him/her* of information obtained.

A central theme of this book is that a well-developed level of information literacy within any individual will necessarily involve a capacity for critical thinking and a degree of metacognitive skill (ie, the individual needs to be capable of consciously reflecting on their own thought processes) in order to undertake such assessments of significance. For 'information literacy', therefore, we should be in the habit of reading 'information literacy and critical thinking', because critical thinking and information literacy go hand-in-hand. There are of course other even more subtle aspects of information, for example, the wide range of 'spoof' items of supposed information and satire available on the world wide web within resources like YouTube. We do not have the space to fully explore such complexities, although it should be noted that the individual who has highly developed critical thinking and metacognitive skills will be in a relatively good position to discriminate literal from satirical sources, and as such a major part of this book can be argued to address that particular subtlety.

1.1.2 Digital Participation in the Information Culture

A major issue for many nations is how best to engage digital technologies in their economic development, public discussion and political engagements. Themes which arise in general discussion and within academic debate include:

- how digital technologies are changing the production, consumption, storage and use of information and knowledge;
- the ethical considerations regarding the Internet;

- how corporate service providers interact with long-standing social institutions like universities, libraries, learned societies, professional bodies;
- how the new media technologies interact with politics, economy, education and social practice;
- what the implications are of the financial crisis for the media industries and the economy and
- the role of media and media education in the information culture.

In addition there is great awareness among the public of specific features of the information culture such as the ubiquity of social media and the Internet. This awareness has been expressed in a variety of forms and narratives. For example:

- the notion of the digital native persona and the particular role of digital technology in education;
- the moral panics over cyber bullying, Internet porn/gambling sites and Internet radicalisation of Jihadis;
- the ethical/political dilemmas and controversies surrounding identity databases, identity cards, intelligence gathering and surveillance (eg, the Snowden/Wikileaks cases, and Freedom of Information legislation);
- the role of social media in political reform (eg, the widespread use of social media during the 2014 Scottish independence Referendum), revolution (Arab Spring) and anticapitalist agitations (The Occupy Movement, The Pirate Party);
- Internet discussion and pressure groups (for example, mumsnet);
- the political and governmental desire for 'digital inclusion' (Scottish/UK and other national policies and projects – Welfare Reform in the UK is a currently live example);
- applications of digital technology to health care, such as websites devoted to providing information about particular conditions giving rise to the construct Health Literacy.

These aspects of the digital information culture raise questions about the institutionalisation of information and knowledge in society and the political economies of nations. They also raise questions about how seriously any current headline item should be taken. This is not straightforward as, for example, Prensky's (2001) idea of 'the digital native' (the younger person who grows up immersed in digital technologies of various kinds, and who is therefore assumed to be thoroughly comfortable with using it), which whilst initially persuasive in some educational circles, has lost traction in academic circles but remains popular in the media and some political circles. All of the above issues are part of our interest in information literacy in the wider population.

In essence, it can be argued that the Internet is now so interrelated with everyday life and the political economy of society, via personal technological devices and their uses, that it is no longer relevant to think in terms of a single *technological entity* (eg, a laptop computer) as the definitive information-handling tool: just as digital information has exploded in the volume of content available, a range of increasingly portable devices such as so-called tablet computers and smartphones, and technologies such as wi-fi for accessing information has developed. As the Internet and digital communications have become ubiquitous and effectively coextensive with society, a social critique is required, which draws on insights from psychology and information literacy. A key question for this book is 'given the ubiquity of the Internet in all matters related to everyday life, what should educators, librarians, researchers, strategic leaders and policy makers do next to ensure that the population are satisfactorily information literate?'

In essence the *information culture* is the information 'landscape' of society as a whole. A modern information culture is a synthesis of all of these aspects and we suggest that information literacy is the functional literacy of such a culture. As noted above, given that the production of Internet resources is massively socially distributed, the notion of social epistemology is critically relevant for everyday use of the Internet, in that it is a key means of gaining critical leverage within that culture.

1.2 INFORMATION LITERACY – A KEY ENABLER OF PARTICIPATION?

The construct *information literacy* (in the sense outlined above of information literacy combined with critical thinking) is a vital enabling factor in ensuring that the benefits of *digital participation* in society, the economy and education are fully realized. The main contention is that when an individual or a society has full information literacy, his/their digital participation will be enhanced, and the potential benefits from Internet use increased. However, without information literacy, the benefits of digital participation will be significantly diminished. In academic terms, information literacy is therefore usefully viewed as an emerging soft applied discipline of the information society and culture (Johnston & Webber, 2006). It is also understood more narrowly by some commentators as a skill set to be developed by students and others, with assistance from teachers and librarians as part of their combined educational efforts. For example, among the lists of skills central to information literacy are the use of the various techniques for accessing sources, formulating searches, and selecting relevant material for a given purpose. This is a perspective which has traditionally been associated with the interests of librarians, teachers, researchers, students and a wide range of professional occupations. There is a growing body of knowledge to guide the practice of all of these groups. However there is growing evidence of wider conceptual frameworks being applied, for example, in ECIL (European Conference on Information Literacy) conferences.

Information literacy is an established, research-based construct and an area of practice in education, public services and workplaces. Information literacy can be defined as follows:

> *Information literacy is the adoption of appropriate information behavior to obtain, through whatever channel or medium, information well fitted to information needs, leading to wise and ethical use of information in society.*
>
> ***Johnston and Webber (2003), p. 336***

This definition includes familiar aspects of information literacy, which can be found in other defining statements, eg, Armstrong et al. (2005) prepared for CILIP, the UK professional body for library and information professionals. In particular the emphasis on searching and finding specific information from a given source, or sources, to meet an identified need are common features across different definitions. Given the library and information profession source of the CILIP definition, it tends to assume that *sources* of information take the form of organised databases, catalogues, indexing and abstracting services and so on, whether hardcopy or online. This of course is still only a narrow selection of information entities, a point which we return to later in this chapter when we discuss our model of the information literacy situation.

The Johnston and Webber definition is distinctive and more holistic in the identification of the more encompassing concept of *information behaviour*, and in identifying the importance of perceiving *appropriate needs* as indicating conscious choice and reflective thinking in a given information *context*. This approach to definition also suggests the reality that information behaviour occurs outside traditional library and information organisations and contexts. For example, people can seek information directly from other people at work, in political parties, social communities, etc.

The definition specifies the sociocultural dimension of information literacy: '…leading to wise and ethical use of information in society'. Thus characterising information literacy in terms of social values, practices and the utility of information for wider social purposes, which influence, and are influenced by, prevailing socioeconomic structures and experiences. There is also within this aspect of the definition a sense that prevailing social structures may be subject to change under the influence of wisdom and ever higher ethical standards.

Becoming information literate is therefore a complex phenomenon, which cannot be adequately achieved by learning a set of practical library or digital skills. There is also a need to learn to think critically and to engage with epistemological development over the life course. Equally, information literacy is not restricted to formal learning situations, it is an integral, if perhaps poorly recognised, part of social, economic and cultural life.

The reference to 'wise and ethical' use of information expresses a broader conceptualisation than one focussing on information access techniques, and aligns more with the interests of specialist researchers and professional advocates of the idea of information literacy as a powerful social force. This includes bodies representing professional librarians and major world organisations such as UNESCO. In virtually all specialist formulations and commentaries information literacy is typically linked to the development of critical thinking and employability; it is also typically seen as an essential aspect of lifelong learning.

A key issue is the degree to which information literacy is explicit/tacit or formal/informal in a given context. Thus, whilst whole populations are evidently living and functioning in an information culture, what is less clear is the extent to which people are aware of this and how able they are to fully engage with information in a critical, metacognitively reflective way. Whilst there are vast quantities of information circulating, particularly in the digital forms of social media and Internet resources, it is not clear how explicit information literacy is as an aspect of the various social phenomena involved.

Under the present conditions of everyday practice, formal education, occupational training, public services, and the current level of technological development, there is no certainty that people will develop the necessary information literacy to fully participate in the online society and information culture of the 21st century. Consequently, information literacy needs to be more fully developed through a variety of contexts in education, workplace activity, communities and participation in lifelong learning generally, in order to maximise social and personal investment in digital technology and services.

These perspectives offer powerful foci for considering the nature of digital inclusion in an information culture and indeed in identifying what some of the benefits and problems might be. However, in addition to the digital informational dimension discussed above, there is another major element that needs to be considered, and that is the psychological aspect of people's use of digital technology. For example, there are issues about how ordinary users conceptualise the world wide web and their use of it, how their ideas affect how they use it, and how their conceptualisations may change through learning. Indeed a major issue for this book is how to improve people's information literacy via learning and teaching interventions.

1.3 PSYCHOLOGY AND PSYCHOLOGICAL INSIGHTS – COGNITION, METACOGNITION AND CRITICAL THINKING

Our approach in this book, therefore, is to consider what the scientific discipline of psychology can tell us about information literacy in formal and informal learning, working life and citizenship in general. Although we do not propose a 'psychology of information literacy' as such, we identify several aspects of psychology, which are relevant to describing information literacy and illuminating relevant learning and teaching.

The standard undergraduate psychology textbook definition of psychology as the science of mind and behaviour will suffice for current purposes, the emphasis within psychology being on the *scientific* (ie, systematic and replicable, often experimental) study of relevant behaviours. In passing we should note the diversity of methodology adopted within psychology; this varies from quantitative, experimental methodologies used in areas like cognitive psychology to more qualitative, observation-based approaches in other areas such as some aspects of social psychology. Our perspective is eclectic as regards methodology: we see each approach as having its strengths and weaknesses and see considerable virtue in mixed-methods approaches which, if done properly, can combine the illuminative insight of the qualitative approaches with the rigour of the experimental, quantitative approach. In the case of information literacy, the relevant behaviours are 'dealing with information' – finding it, selecting among items of it, making sense of it, and making decisions on the basis of it. This implicates many different areas of psychology, for example:

- Problem-solving: having decided that there is an informational need, obtaining just the right information can be construed as a kind of problem-solving. The literature on classical problem-solving in psychology suggests various pathologies of thinking, such as underexploration of the problem space, perseveration, and confirmation bias that could well operate in information literacy situations.

- Comprehension: making sense of text and images is a psychological problem of no small complexity, and there is a massive research literature within psychology on such topics as text comprehension. For the purposes of this book we do not delve into the details of low-level language comprehension processes but assume a reasonable (average or better than average) level of skill in this area on the part of the user.
- Critical thinking: deciding whether to believe or take seriously an information source implicates a capacity to think critically. Some research within psychology has raised serious questions about the extent to which we typically think critically (or not) and about how to improve people's critical thinking skills. This is a major focus for Chapter 3 of this book.
- Developmental psychology: to the extent that children think differently from adults, the study of how children, adolescents and adults vary in tasks involving information searching and handling should link to phenomena noted in the developmental psychology literature. We touch on this issue in various places, but most particularly within Chapter 5.
- Learning: related though not identical to the issue immediately above, how do we learn to deal with information? Again, this is examined in Chapter 5.
- Personality: Heinstrom (2010) reports studies on how personality affects the processes of online searching. In order to keep the current volume to a manageable length, we do not explore this particular issue but instead provide broad generalisations regarding pedagogy and learning; the interested reader could then examine Heinstrom's work to explore the extent to which the broad principles that we adduce should be qualified by reference to the effect of individual differences on searching strategies.
- Social psychology: given that other people are often the sources of information, the whole issue of authority, provenance, trustworthiness and so on are implicated – that is, social epistemology. This concept is explored more fully in Chapter 9 but for the moment we should note that the phenomena that we are focussing on implicate a social dimension to major epistemological questions.

To attempt to cover all of the above territory would in effect be to write a psychology textbook, which is not our purpose. Our coverage of psychological themes is therefore selective. We don't, for example, for reasons of space directly review the classic literature on problem solving which focuses on the solution of so-called 'well-formed' problems such as puzzles and games and tries to identify common shortcomings in people's problem-solving efforts. However, the material that we do discuss (constructivism, pedagogies and metacognition) should provide ways of avoiding the pathologies of problem-solving identified in the classical problem-solving literature (such as 'confirmation bias' and underexploration of the problem space, which can be ameliorated via metacognitive monitoring and critical thinking during the course of problem-solving activities).

Our account of information literacy treats it as a social phenomenon experienced in the lives of:

- Citizens, teachers, learners, librarians, educational developers, digital technologists and those in a variety of other roles, for example in the workplace or as hobbyists.

Additionally, information literacy is relevant to information channels and particular media such as:

- Print publications, video productions and libraries
- Internet resources and search engines
- Social media
- Television programmes.

All of the above might be regarded as *psychological and cultural tools*, in the sense of being both extensions of mind and forms of action in society (Hutchins, 1995), whilst simultaneously existing as cultural artefacts or 'containers' of knowledge that has been produced by given social/psychological activity systems. A given 'tool' such as writing, or a diagram, can exist at both the individual and small group levels of a 'classroom', the intermediate level of a library or website and the cultural level of social production, consumption and conservation of information/knowledge. From this perspective it becomes possible to see the cultural in the quotidian and to look through a given learning situation as a lens with which to view the cultural whole of a society.

1.4 CONCLUSION AND STRUCTURE OF THE BOOK

Ultimately, however, in the face of the multitude of information sources available electronically and in print, the individual is confronted with the dilemma of how to decide which particular information contents to accept as (in some sense) true, and which sources of information to regard as trustworthy. As is more fully discussed in Chapter 4, this raises the issue of lay epistemology (ie, the individual's conception of the nature of knowledge and of how to decide on what is true and to be believed). It also, given that a great deal of our knowledge ultimately relies upon the expertise and trustworthiness of others, raises the issue of lay social epistemology, which is more fully discussed in Chapter 9. As Chapter 4 indicates, psychological research has documented the variety of epistemological ideas that people can hold, varying from a simple, binary, black-and-white view of knowledge as falling cleanly into the categories of 'right' and 'wrong' on the one hand, to a much more relativistic conception in which all knowledge is viewed as ultimately uncertain to a degree, but with some aspects much better supported by evidence and therefore inherently more trustworthy. We argue that the different epistemological positions affect the individual's approach to the issue of selecting information sources. Further complexity is added to the individual's decision-making process when the social origin of much information is considered: under what circumstances is the individual justified in accepting the statements, opinions and claims of others as being true? This issue is more fully addressed in Chapter 9, but for now we note that the individual who is confronted by a particular item of information (a web page, for example) has to consider both the believability of the content in terms of how convincingly it is argued and supported by evidence (epistemological questions) and also how trustworthy is its provenance (What are the qualifications of the originator of the information? Does he/she have a vested interest in having people believe the content of the website? and so on – clear examples of social epistemological questions).

Given the possibility (which receives a good deal of empirical support in the psychology literature, see Chapter 4) that individuals' epistemological ideas are subject to change over time and in particular open to improvement as a function of educational interventions, this immediately raises questions about pedagogies for improving epistemology, social epistemology and critical thinking.

Chapter 2 summarises our case study, which examined information literacy in a group of adults who were on a part-time course designed to help them return to full-time study at undergraduate level following a post-school period of full-time work. This study suggested a number of conclusions, and in particular that this group of learners was prone to holding a categorical, 'right' versus 'wrong' view of knowledge which located information as being 'in' the text and rendered some sources (textbooks) as inherently reliable and other sources (websites) as inherently less reliable. Arguably these epistemological views represent a 'common sense' reaction to the notion of information in an educational setting. Viewed from the perspective of the literature on student learning in higher education, such naive adult learner perceptions could be explained in terms of the various suboptimal approaches to learning/critical thinking identified within that literature.

The data obtained in the case study imply that it would be beneficial to help the learners to develop better and more complex understandings of learning and information, with information literacy as a key element of their approach to learning. This leads us to consider in Section B of the book what we believe to be the key psychological capabilities that underpin the development of information literacy: epistemological development (Chapter 3), metacognition (ie, the capacity to reflect upon and consciously regulate one's own thought processes; Chapter 4) and the plethora of phenomena related to learning (Chapter 5). We use the insights gleaned from a consideration of these bodies of literature to suggest changes to the design of courses and a review of their pedagogical practice in the light of the research literature. We do not endorse any single policy, technology or activity as a panacea for the problems that we consider, but adopt an altogether more nuanced approach to the re-design. However, there is some virtue in trying to identify 'high-impact' information and learning activities, which might provide a basis for substantial practical development.

These considerations lead us to examine in Section C some prominent contributions from the Library and Information Science (LIS) community and in particular the recent revisions to the Association of College and Research Libraries (ACRL) standards are arguably linked to recent pedagogical developments within US higher education (Chapter 7); Secker and Coonan Curriculum for Information Literacy (Chapter 6); and UNESCO statements on Information Literacy, and Media and Information Literacy together with recent work on the knowledge society (Chapter 8). The book concludes with an account of the notion of social epistemology, which draws all the strands together and draws out some suggestions for curriculum development and teaching methods (Chapter 9).

For the moment though, we will conclude this introductory chapter by outlining the features of a generic model of the information literacy situation involving a person, an information entity such as a book, leaflet or website, a relevant subject matter area (the topic of the information purveyed by the information entity), and a context within which the information literacy situation is happening. Note that from the outset we emphasise information literacy *situations* rather than information literacy as some sort of property of the individual involved, because we believe the context, the subject matter area and the nature of the information literacy entity all combine to affect information literacy behaviour and are key to persons becoming information-literate. This very much echoes the discussion in the Preface of Schwartz, Neuman, Gil, and Ilya's (2003) activity perspective on argumentative reasoning, and our adoption of a situated activity perspective on information literacy.

Fig. 1.1 above shows the initial diagram of our generic information literacy model. This is intended as a general characterisation of information literacy situations, including both educational ones and also workplace and citizenship-related examples. Several aspects of the model require immediate comment and further explanation.

The core of the model has four elements – the person involved, the context in which information literacy is relevant, the information entity under consideration, and the relevant subject matter area. Each of these elements requires further elaboration, and we do that both here and also by considering the model again in a more detailed way in later chapters of the book. It is noteworthy that we see information literacy as involving all four of these elements in interaction with one another, rather than characterising information literacy as a 'skill' possessed by and internal to an individual. Information literacy is a relational, contextualised phenomenon which will manifest itself in a particular way as a function of the interaction of all four elements with each other. Change one (eg, the context) in some way and you will in all likelihood change the information literacy behaviour displayed.

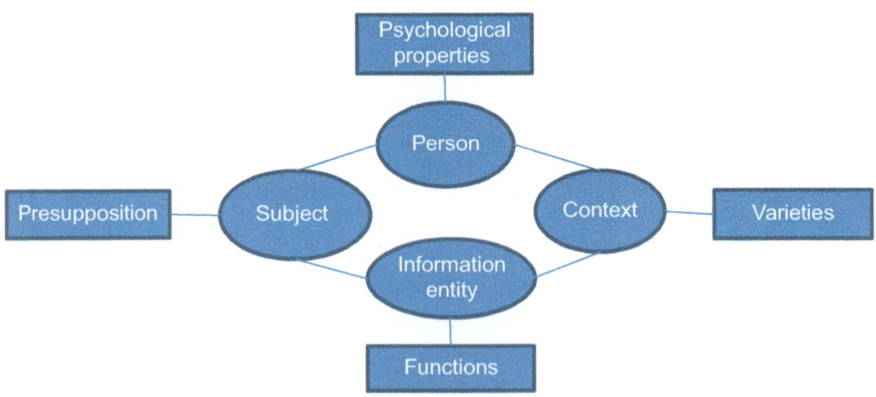

Figure 1.1 Initial model of the information literacy situation.

The 'person' element is of course a very variable entity: persons vary greatly in terms of (for example) their age, experience, occupation and educational status, not to mention a host of other psychological variables, all of which will have implications for their performance of information-literacy-related activities. A considerable proportion of this book is devoted to explicating the implications of key psychological variables for information literacy. For this initial specification of the model, though, we simply link the node 'psychological properties' to the 'person' element as a shorthand for all of these variables. But, for example, the person's relevant prior knowledge, their capacity for critical thinking, their epistemology, their degree of metacognitive skill, and their motivation and disposition to think thoroughly about an information entity will all influence how they perform on an information literacy task.

The 'context' element reflects the fact that information literacy activities do not take place in a vacuum but in relation to other human purposes and activities. A variety of contexts exist; to take but four examples, educational contexts, the workplace, leisure activities such as hobby-related contexts and citizenship activities (such as deciding how to cast one's vote in an election) all represent quite distinct contexts in which information literacy activities can take place. These in turn will have an influence upon the information literacy activities that do take place; for example, the person might be very concerned to access up-to-date and accurate information in a work or educational context, but rather less concerned about these properties of information in a hobby-related context. There are, of course, other aspects of the context that will have effects on information literacy behaviours – for example, whether the person is undertaking their information literacy activity alone or as part of a dyad or group (as he/she might do, for example, in some educational contexts).

The information entity element can take a variety of forms – for example, it might be a book or website that a learner is reading, it might be a piece of software like a search engine (which is also an information entity by virtue of its presentation of icons, text and check boxes and so on for the user to interact with), it might be a political party election manifesto pamphlet, or it might even be an information entity that the person is trying to produce, such as, for example, a student writing an essay. Attached to that element is the node labelled 'functions' to underscore that a variety of purposes can be attached to an information entity – for example, it might be designed to persuade the person of a particular point of view, or alternatively it might be intended to entertain, or to provoke thought, or quite possibly combinations of these and other purposes. If it is an information entity that the person themselves are producing, it could again serve a number of functions or purposes – to persuade, to impress, to gain high marks and so on. This variety of purposes and functions will again exert an influence on how the person carries out an information literacy activity.

The subject matter element relates to the content of the information. For example, it might be related to an academic subject such as chemistry, or the views of a political party. In both cases, it will be associated with a set of beliefs (here represented by a linked node in the model) or what might loosely be termed presuppositions; in the case of chemistry this might take the form of the widespread acceptance of such things as the atomic theory of matter and the scientific method as the preferred means of enquiry, whereas in the case of the political pamphlet this might take the form of a core set of beliefs about how much the state should actively run people's lives, how large and inclusive the welfare state should be and so on.

It should be noted that there is no direct link in the model from 'person' to 'information entity'. In one sense there is very obviously a direct link in that people physically handle and read books, write on paper and scroll through computer screens, for example. However, we contend that even though there is such direct physical contact, the context and knowledge about the subject matter are in effect lenses through which the information entity is always viewed, and the person's interaction with the information entity is always constrained by these two elements. Hence there is no direct link between person and information entity within the model.

As we go through the chapters within this book we will elaborate each of these nodes (psychological properties of persons, varieties of contexts, forms, functions and purposes of information entities, and presuppositions within particular subject matter areas) in various ways to highlight their effects on information literacy behaviour, but we would conclude for the moment with our firm contention that the proper way to conceptualise information literacy is as an interaction among the four core elements. This, we argue, will have implications for how we might go about changing people's information literacy behaviours.

CHAPTER 2

Information Literacy in Adult Returner Students: The Pre-Entry Class Case Study

Research with adult returners to higher education is presented as an example of the complex of approaches to information and learning potentially present in the wider population. Results indicate a low level of information literacy amongst the returners accompanied by a limited development of the study skills and critical thinking required for degree-level study. A corroborative study of psychology students is presented, which indicates comparable limitations in terms of critical thinking and information literacy. The research studies illuminate the need to improve pedagogical strategies and teaching practices within the design of university studies.

2.1 THE BACKGROUND CONTEXT

The Scottish Bachelor-level degree is relatively unusual within the UK context in that it takes four years rather than three for students to complete an Honours degree. Another relatively unusual feature in a UK context is that Scottish Bachelor degrees, particularly but not exclusively those in the Arts, Humanities and the Social Sciences, are initially broad-based. Thus, the student may commence his or her studies with the intention of graduating with a single honours degree in a specific academic subject, but he/she will have to study three academic subjects including their desired subject during first year, followed by two subjects including the desired subject in second year, before concentrating solely on the desired subject for the third and fourth years. This same degree structure (initially broad, but more narrow in the later years of study) is true for degrees in all academic subjects in the above group of degrees (except in the case of joint honours degrees, where two subjects continue to be studied in third and fourth years). This broad curriculum in first year has implications for the design of any access courses; in the interest of letting the students know what first year is going to be like, breadth of coverage is advisable.

Copyright © 2016 A. Anderson and B. Johnston.
Published by Elsevier Ltd.
All rights reserved.

From Information Literacy to Social Epistemology
ISBN 978-0-08-100545-3

The study that we undertook (Anderson, Johnston, & MacDonald, 2013) examined the experiences of students on a particular access course, the Pre-Entry Access Course in Arts and Social Sciences at the University of Strathclyde. This course offers potential adult returners the opportunity to study part-time a variety of arts and social sciences subjects as a prelude to possibly re-entering full-time education as an undergraduate student in either arts subjects (typically languages), social sciences, some business subjects and the LLB degree in Law. A sufficiently strong performance on the pre-entry course is recognised as meeting entry requirements for admission to undergraduate degree study; at the time of writing, entry to all of the undergraduate courses listed above is highly competitive and good marks (60–70% average across the pre-entry modules studied) are required for admission to the courses listed.

The course is open to adult returner applicants, a group who are defined as having been away from full-time formal education for a period of at least 3 years (which means that this group of students are typically at least 21 years old, and in effect are the group formerly referred to as 'mature students'). In practice, a range of individuals of different ages and from equally varied backgrounds apply to this course. At one extreme, this includes young adults who are either unemployed and who perceive a degree as a route into a career, or individuals who are already in occupations but who would like to obtain a degree as a vehicle for effecting a career change. At the other extreme, it includes retired individuals who are fulfilling a long-harboured ambition to undertake academic study that circumstances had in one way or another denied to them earlier in their lives. Like many equivalent access courses run by other institutions, the pre-entry access course at Strathclyde allows students to sample the higher education experience and, if they wish, to use the course as a vehicle for getting onto a full-time degree course, either at Strathclyde or at any of a number of other universities that recognise the pre-entry access course for admissions purposes. Equally, having sampled the higher education experience, pre-entry course students are free not to proceed forward to undergraduate study if they wish. As a part-time course taught by evening study, it is particularly attractive to individuals who are in full-time work who wish to tentatively explore university-level study without committing themselves to a full-time access course, with all the implications of sacrifice and financial hardship that the latter might entail.

Like the first year of the undergraduate degree to which the pre-entry course feeds in, it involves the study of three academic subjects. These are taught in a series of three modules of seven teaching weeks' duration, interspersed with generic sessions on study skills, applying through UCAS (the United Kingdom's Universities and Colleges Admissions System) and so on, meaning that the three subjects chosen are covered in succession (unlike the undergraduate degree proper, where the three subjects are covered simultaneously). The course therefore strikes a compromise in that the breadth of subjects studied in the first year of the degree proper is replicated, but in a less demanding timetable that allows exclusive concentration on one academic subject at a time, as befits a course which is preparing individuals who have not been engaged in full-time study for some time, for the subsequent more intensive undergraduate first year. The range of modules on offer draws upon the range of subjects taught within the BA (Humanities and Social Sciences) curriculum and in many cases involves the same teaching staff as the students will encounter if they proceed forward to first-year full-time undergraduate study.

It is worth considering at this point what information literacy tasks are inherent in a course such as the pre-entry course. The course requires students to attend lectures and to support the learning accrued from that context with the aid of background reading. Additional learning tasks such as essay writing require the student to seek out material on a particular theme, to summarise what the relevant body of academic literature claims, and ideally to subject these academic/theoretical ideas to appropriate criticism. Such activities entail a number of recognisable facets of information literacy, and in particular obtaining, processing, synthesising and critically evaluating material that may originate within a number of diverse sources. The students themselves are primarily full-time employees in workaday occupations such as the retail sector, local government and so on, and only secondarily are students. As such they are as a sample reasonably representative of the general population. This raises questions concerning the information literacy history of the students, which one can surmise will be likely to be somewhat varied. For example, different occupational contexts will entail varying amounts of usage of IT equipment for the purposes of obtaining information, and variation in the extent to which any information retrieved requires interpretation or critique. All of the students can be expected to have the right to access public libraries but again the extent to which doing so is habitual for them will vary from individual to individual. The fundamental learning and information literacy tasks will therefore be likely to be fairly familiar to some of the students but less so to others, and their first experience of studying in a higher education context might to some students at least be something of a revelation; we will explore this point more fully in Chapter 6 when we discuss transformational learning.

2.2 THE STUDY ITSELF

A swathe of research literature indicates that there exist shortcomings in students' information literacy skills, both in terms of use of a suboptimal set of information search strategies and in terms of evaluating the quality of the information found by searches (eg, Brem, Russell, & Weems, 2001; Halverson, Siegel, & Freyermuth, 2010; Jansen, Spink, & Saracevic, 2000; Lazonder, 2000; Nicholas, Huntington, Williams, & Dobrowolski, 2006). For example, Halverson et al. (2010) found that the criteria which students used to evaluate and select information included both relevant (eg, the information's credibility and accuracy) and nonrelevant (eg, the information's readability and its superficial aesthetic features) criteria. Similarly, Attar (2005) conducted interviews with adult participants whilst they accessed and used web pages, to investigate adults' use of and reaction to websites. Attar observed a number of problems in the way his participants dealt with information, such as uncertainty on the part of some users as to whether a given page was an 'official' organisational site or a page written by an individual.

The studies discussed above suggest that one might reasonably anticipate weaknesses in people's information literacy skills. We therefore launched a qualitative study examining the participants' perceptions of information use. In particular we wanted to know the reasons people give for the information selection choices that they make. We therefore conducted open-ended, semistructured interviews on three broad themes with a sample of volunteers from the pre-entry course cohort: students' experiences of study in the access course thus far, students' approaches to studying, and students' information literacy. The interviews were conducted on our behalf by three postgraduate students experienced in semistructured interviewing; their instructions were to get the participants talking on each of the three broad themes listed above, and the subsequent data were transcribed and qualitatively analysed via extraction of common themes across participants. We did not mention to the postgraduate students conducting the interviews any theory or terminology associated with information literacy so that none of that terminology was used by the interviewers, to minimise the risk of our distorting the participants' responses. Participants were simply asked questions about how they went about finding desired information and how they selected particular books or articles from among the results obtained, for further study. A similar study was carried out by Whitmire (2003), using Yale undergraduates as participants. However, our study involved a broader scope of questioning than did Whitmire's, which allowed us to relate information literacy to broader issues such as study skills (Anderson, Johnston, & McDonald, 2011; Anderson, McDonald, & Johnston, 2011). Additionally, our study involved adult returners rather than senior undergraduates. Nevertheless, there are interesting parallels between the two studies.

Eighteen volunteer individuals (nine male, nine female, of varied ages, with all participants older than 21 years of age and with a maximum age of 70 for one participant) were interviewed. Their responses were transcribed and subsequently qualitatively analysed using the constant comparative method (Glaser, 1992; Strauss & Corbin, 1990) to extract themes that were commonly in evidence across the participants' responses. As already indicated, students commented not just on information searching activities, but also on how they went about studying material and in more general terms on how the course was going for them. We therefore discuss each of these areas in turn.

2.2.1 Information Literacy

Our findings in respect of information literacy can be summarised under two headings: (1) finding and using sources, and (2) deciding on the trustworthiness of sources.

2.2.1.1 Finding and Using Sources

In this area of information literacy activity, our respondents had a number of purposes, for example (and primarily) to obtain more information relevant to material that they had encountered in lectures, to find information that they could use within their course assignments, and more generally to broaden their knowledge of an academic subject via 'background' reading. Students showed a strong tendency to treat recommended textbooks as their primary source of information, whereas the Internet tended to be used as a backup to find supplementary materials. They described themselves as tending to focus on what they deemed to be the relevant parts of textbooks, sampling from perhaps several textbooks and explicitly avoiding reading entire books. This could reflect a learning strategy of covering the bare minimum for the purposes at hand, or it could be a strategy for avoiding digression. The students tended to be hazy about the bases on which they made judgements concerning how much reading was sufficient for their purposes.

They also reported seeking help to identify relevant texts from a number of sources: their university tutors (on occasion, though some expressed a reluctance to seek such help on the grounds that they ought to be able to do it themselves), their local public library, the university library staff, and family members who were themselves students, but interestingly, not their classmates.

2.2.1.2 Deciding on the Trustworthiness of Sources

As noted above, textbooks were perceived as reliable and trustworthy sources of information in a way that internet sources were not necessarily so, and this is exemplified by the following quote:

> *'Well the internet I was a bit wary about because obviously on the different websites and things if its published in a book then you're a bit more confident thinking that this is actually kind of true information, whereas when I was looking at different websites, I mean there were some that were just wacky and I was just like I'm just not even going to let that sink into my brain in case I start talking about it'*
>
> ***Anderson et al. (2013)***

This presupposes a clear distinction between 'true' and (implicitly) false information, which could be argued to reflect a 'dualist' or 'realist' epistemology in which information divides into two clearly distinguishable categories, characterised by one of our participants as 'facts' versus 'conjecture'. The research literature on epistemological thinking and its relevance to information literacy is discussed further in Chapter 4. As an aside it is worth noting that one effect of this dualistic thinking was a reluctance to engage in peer interaction, because fellow students' knowledge was perceived as less valuable than that possessed by tutors, and students failed to see the point of hearing about their fellow students' views. To paraphrase one student, peer interaction sessions were seen as a waste of time; the time would have been better spent listening to the lecturer (ie, an 'expert').

The second finding that emerged from the students' comments is that they are unclear as to how they make decisions regarding the relevance of particular sources, making frequent use of phrases like '...I am not exactly sure...' or '...you just know..' (without being able to articulate how). One respondent went so far as to claim that 'you automatically, subconsciously' look out for signs that tell you whether a source is trustworthy or not, 'but don't realise it...I think you just know'.

The interview data suggest that these respondents subscribe to a 'sources' concept of information, with a strong sense of reliance on the authority of staff and published texts, which fits with the distinction noted above between facts and conjecture. This led to students cautiously 'sticking to the rules' about what is legitimate information activity, and these rules in turn were inferred from what staff said about information searching. Interviewees' responses suggested that they had a developing sense of how to form judgements about subject-related sources of information for study purposes. This tended to be somewhat rudimentary, relying substantially on consensus across sources in the absence of explicit articulated criteria and the notion of 'authority'. For example the quote cited above also has implications for critical thinking:

> *'Well the internet I was a bit wary about because obviously on the different websites and things if its published in a book then you're a bit more confident thinking that this is actually kind of true information, whereas when I was looking at different websites, I mean there were some that were just wacky and I was just like I'm just not even going to let that sink into my brain in case I start talking about it'*

As noted in Anderson et al. (2013), the above quote also highlights how unconfident students are regarding their own critical faculties, otherwise the risk of 'wacky' information 'sinking into (one's) brain' would be minimal.

2.2.2 Patterns of Learning

The literature on patterns of learning is reviewed in more detail in Chapter 5. For the present purposes, a thumbnail summary will suffice to help to contextualise our participants' comments on the issue of approaches to study. Whereas earlier and very well-known literature had drawn a now well-known distinction between 'deep' (meaning-oriented) and 'surface' (memorisation-oriented) 'approaches to' learning (eg, Biggs, 1987; Entwistle, 2001, 2007; Marton & Säljö, 1997), a more complex conceptualisation has since evolved. Vermunt (2007) describes broad 'patterns' of learning, each of which is associated with a particular processing strategy, a regulation strategy, a particular conception of learning and a learning orientation. The four patterns of learning that he identifies are named undirected (which is characterised by a lack of regulation and a degree of passivity), reproduction-directed (which involves a processing strategy that uses memorising and analysing, assumes external regulation, conceptualises learning as receiving transmitted knowledge and is test-oriented), meaning-directed (which involves 'deep' processing, self-regulation and conceptualises learning as knowledge construction) and finally application-directed (which involves an application-oriented processing strategy, a combination of self- and external regulation, conceptualises learning as using knowledge, and is vocationally oriented). The reproduction-directed and the meaning-directed patterns correspond to the former 'surface' and 'deep' approaches to learning, respectively, whilst the undirected and application-directed correspond to two extremes of strategic approaches.

The participants in our study reported using fairly rudimentary study techniques, which typically involved multiple readings of textbooks. For example, to quote one student,

> *'I don't know if what I am doing is right, I just read the information, I write it down, I read it again, I write it down. I just try and write it down and read it as much as possible so that hopefully some of it sticks.'*

More rarely, such reading is combined with integration of other materials. More rarely still a variety of learning strategies is selected among, with reference to the demands that particular academic disciplines place on learning. For example:

> *'Well Sociology was just re-writing notes that I had taken in class about the relevant material and reading books. In Spanish I put my words on cards and labelled everything in my house and put signs up on my wall. For Law again I just wrote out quotations and did mind maps for the little Acts and quotes. I've been in education for some time so I've picked up a few things along the way.'*

These study techniques appear to be used very much in the service of a reproduction-directed pattern of learning, with the aim of rote memorisation of information and frequent reference to getting information to 'stick' in the mind. The interviewees are arguably reporting making an effort to retain or remember the material, but they don't show any evidence of having explicitly incorporated any of the study skills techniques that have been made available to them. Neither do they show any evidence of deliberately adopting 'deep' processing strategies such as attempting to obtain overviews of the material or trying to learn relationships between elements within the subject matter being studied. O'Donnell and Tobell (2007) conducted an interview study with students on a similar access course to that which our participants were taking, and found that their interviewees appeared to prefer to use their own study methods as opposed to adopting study skills advice from their tutors. In the case of one of O'Donnell and Tobell's participants, the participant explicitly rejected study skills advice. Both our interviewees and those of O'Donnell and Tobell appear to prefer a 'learning through doing' approach to studying.

Again, as was the case with issues relating to information literacy (see above), respondents report seeking advice on study-related matters from relatives who had experience of studying in higher education:

> *'It's 30 years since I left school so I wasn't really confident about (writing essays). Fortunately, not only did I have the help of the tutors here but my daughter is about to go to (another University) to do Law. So she kept me straight and I bought the books at the start to get the structure.' (Interview C3)*

Anderson, Johnston, and MacDonald (2012).

In summary, several findings relevant to patterns of study emerged from these interviews. First, the most common processing strategy reported by participants was the fairly rudimentary study technique of reading textbooks repeatedly, sometimes integrating their content with those of other materials, and more rarely still participants report the use of a variety of learning strategies selected with reference to the demands that particular academic disciplines place on learning. These learning techniques appear to be used in the service of a surface or reproductive approach to learning. Second, there is evidence of realist and more rarely multiplist epistemologies among these students, as might be anticipated from the research literature on epistemological development in students. These epistemologies in turn will be likely to influence study strategy. Third, students expressed scepticism regarding the value of peer interaction, and a reluctance to engage with it. This wariness seemed to stem from multiple sources such as epistemological views that fellow students' knowledge would be less valuable than tutors', and issues of self-confidence.

2.2.3 Transformational Learning

The research literature on transformational learning is reviewed more fully in Chapter 6. Briefly, the theory of transformational learning concerns an individual's values, beliefs and assumptions, which constitute a lens through which 'personal experience is mediated and made sense of' (Merriam, 2004, p. 62). When individuals find they can no longer use these values and beliefs to make sense of an experience, transformational learning can occur to allow the development of a new perspective which is 'more inclusive, discriminating, open and reflective'; in short, more developed (Mezirow, 2000). Mezirow's original (1974) study of women being emancipated by return to college study after years in the workplace or of raising a family, is seminal. Participants reported that the experience of college had changed them significantly, in ways that fundamentally affected how they thought about the world.

In respect of transformational learning, the interview data from our students arguably provide some evidence of transformation in learners' perceptions of themselves as a function of having undertaken access course study. For example, interviewees reported becoming more analytical in their day-to-day thinking, and of coming to see the learning process, and not just the end product, as important for them; such changes in perspective fit very well with Mezirow's notion of transformation. To quote one interviewee:

> *'It has really changed me though in the way I think about uni it was more the idea of doing, getting a degree but now it's more I actually can learn something and I*

can I don't know do more with the whole uni experience I think that it has changed me that way, it's given me more commitment and you know I'm more focused and I'm more disciplined in a way because you only had seven weeks to get something down and you had such a short time span to learn so much things so in a way you had to discipline yourself if you wanted it..... I think it's definitely been beneficial and it's changed me a bit.'

The interviews also reveal that the students had held specific presuppositions regarding study in higher education, which were contradicted by the actual experience, in that the access course provided a more diverse range of teaching and learning experiences than the anticipated exclusivity of lectures, and in not involving sarcasm toward or belittling of students during teaching sessions:

'Well before I was, before I was coming here I was rather apprehensive just about whether or not this was a good thing or a bad thing, but you forget how open people can be especially those who are teaching to those who are wanting to learn. There's a sort of informal, unwritten rule that you're not going to be made fun of because you're learning, we all want to learn...'

Several interviewees reflected on their time in the course and suggested that the experience of taking part in it had changed them in noticeable ways:

'...It has certainly made me in the last 7 or 8 months been much more of a bookworm. I've found myself not only just reading academic books but things of that period of that particular subject to link with it, so I'm certainly reading a lot more and I've adapted my lifestyle to be committed to actually doing some study work on a regular basis, so my lifestyle has changed to that extent...' (Interview C3)

'Certainly yes I do feel I've changed yes. I'm starting to think more object, how do you say it... I used to jump into situations where I'm looking more analytically now whether it be even in my work or whatever, because when you've been out of education for that period of time then you tend to get into a rut and I think challenging yourselves a good way to move forward through that to be honest. Yes certainly.' (Interview R5)

The above comment hints at an interesting transfer of what is learned (objective, analytical thinking) to arenas beyond university work.

'I think I have became more confident in myself because I'm very much like go to my work everyday to do the same thing everyday whereas now I kind of feel myself kind of broadening out a little bit and wanting to learn and wanting to do better and I think basically I just want to just I know I'm still young and everything but I was just like, I wanted to have a better life than, obviously I've got quite a good job and it's a nice shop and things but I just thought there's only so far you can go in retail and I

thought you know I've always wanted to kind of push myself that little bit further so yes so.' (Interview R4)

We would argue that our participants' interviews do occasionally show evidence of transformational learning, one example being a transformation from seeing the product of learning as critical to one of seeing the process of learning as critical. This is arguably a key element in students' understanding of learning: their initial outcome-orientated focus is arguably nontransformational, in contrast to their later metacognitive awareness of learning as a process, which is transformational in quality. There was also evidence that transformation affected not just the participants' view of learning, but also affected how they thought about other areas of their lives (with participants claiming that they approached problems more objectively and analytically), and was associated with growth in self-confidence as a learner, and an increasing degree of focus and self-discipline.

2.3 SUMMARY

The overall picture of the access course student at the end of their access course that emerges from this sample of interviews is one where typically the individual has fairly rudimentary study skills and information literacy skills, allied to a realist epistemology in which there are right and wrong answers to academic questions. They see it as their task to learn the 'right' answers rather than opinions or conjecture and therefore focus on learning from textbooks on the grounds that, being published in book form, their contents have been vetted and are more dependable. These students expect to encounter mainly lecturing-based teaching and learning experiences. This sample of access students typically report feeling academically underconfident and have anxieties about looking foolish before their peers during the course of teaching and learning. Nevertheless, these interviewees sometimes report having been transformed in significant ways by the experience of having taken the access course.

2.4 CORROBORATIVE STUDIES

Jones and Allen (2012) examined the library skills and experiences of psychology undergraduate students across two institutions by running a number of focus groups involving a total of 38 students. In the focus groups they explored such issues as: the students' information skills and search strategies, their use of the wide range of available information sources, how they evaluate information sources, the specific problems and successes that students encounter when using library resources, how they tried to deal with the difficulties they encountered, and students' views on how best to improve their academic information literacy. Jones (personal communication) confirmed that their sample was drawn from a range of year groups and, one assumes, who entered university from a variety of backgrounds (school, college) as compared to our own study which was specifically of adult returner students who were at the time of the research still taking their access course, albeit one based within the university. Despite these differences, Jones and Allen report a series of findings very much in line with our own.

Thematic analysis of the students' responses revealed a number of interesting findings:

- The students' studies undertaken prior to the degree were highly prescriptive with everything required for study (which in practice was typically a limited range of materials) supplied by the teacher.
- Students regarded books as reliable compared to Internet sources and evaluated sources in terms of their apparent relevance to the assignment being undertaken, with some differentiation among websites based on their provenance, eg, websites with URL addresses ending in .gov being regarded as more reliable, and Wikipedia for example being somewhat distrusted.
- Students reported feeling overwhelmed by the sheer volume of resources that are available in the typical university library compared to the typical school or college library, feeling less supported in university than in college or school, and acutely aware that the expectations of them at university were somewhat more demanding than had been the case at school.
- Standalone library induction sessions were felt to be less useful than sessions that had been integrated into their course of study.
- Students recognised that journal articles were more likely to be up-to-date than books but had uncertainties regarding how best to search for the most appropriate journal articles for their purpose, in terms of what keywords to use.
- Whilst students are encouraged by tutors to 'read around' an area, students are quite uncertain what this means in terms of where to start and how many journal articles to use, and there is evidence that the complexity of journal articles is confusing for them.

Jones and Allen concluded that when designing information literacy instruction for students it is important to know about the types of information that they had to deal with in their studies prior to their degree course, that IL instruction is best integrated within academic curricula and that students are given full explanations of the variety of journals (eg, full-text versus abstract only) that are available. Interestingly, in relation to our own emphasis within the present book, they argue for the inclusion of peer support and collaborative learning within any IL instruction.

It is also worth noting that the study by Jones and Allen is not the only one that corroborates our findings: Whitmire (2003) observed similar phenomena in Yale undergraduates to those noted here. Whitmire's work involved interviewing a sample of Yale undergraduates about their information search processes as they completed a research paper during the course of their final year, and, for example, showed that the Yale students demonstrated the same preference for textbooks over other sources that our students did. Hofer (2004) likewise obtained similar findings; Hofer's work is discussed more fully in Chapter 4. The point to be emphasised though is that our findings are corroborated by similar studies undertaken with other groups of students elsewhere.

2.5 CONCLUSIONS

It is interesting that both our own case study and others in the literature point to a similar set of phenomena: weaknesses in information literacy processes thanks to a number of characteristics:

- presumptions on the part of the students regarding the reliability of different types of information sources;
- weaknesses in students' awareness and control over their own thought processes ('metacognition'; see Chapter 4) leading to uncertainty regarding how to judge such issues as the quality of information and the sufficiency of the amount of it obtained;
- the importance of contextual factors such as the availability to students of more information literate others, such as relatives.

It is perhaps worth reiterating that our sample of students, who were all part-time students and most of whom had full-time daytime employment (in such roles as, for example, police officers, shopworkers and firefighters), constitute a sample that is somewhat closer to being a sample of the general public than is the case for many studies in psychology, which tend to use younger full-time undergraduate students as participants. The attendance of this group of more mature individuals at university brings 'information' (ie, the concept of content that has to have its veracity explicitly judged) to their attention in perhaps a more explicit way than they will have experienced before.

Returning to our model of the information literacy situation (see Chapter 1) and reconsidering the pre-entry course students' activities in the light of that model, we note that the model identifies particular *information entities*, such as **essays**, where learning, subject knowledge, information activities and critical thinking intersect (although they do not always enjoy a proportionate amount of attention). For example, a student's essay will typically be judged on grounds of the characteristics and quality of critical thinking demonstrated by the student writer. To that end an important aspect of the essay-writing task will be the extent and nature of student engagement with relevant literature. The academic literature drawn upon by the student typically reflects different and possibly conflicting perspectives within the discipline concerning the specific topic of the essay and therefore presents the student with the need to make choices between disciplinary perspectives, which are both relevant to the essay topic and justifiable in terms of a particular argument within their essay. As noted above, the students' perspective of seeking 'true' or 'correct' material conflicts with the possibility of more than one information source being worthy of consideration.

Where does this literature come from? One obvious source is a reading list provided by the lecturer as a guide to student reading. In many cases a reading list will be indicative rather than comprehensive, thereby encouraging the student to go beyond the reading list to the Internet perhaps or indeed the library. This factual possibility raises the other source of literature – that is identified by the student as part of their research into the essay topic. It is this latter source, which tends to be associated with the classical accounts of IL presented here as:

- knowledge of sources;
- identification of search terms;
- iterative search process;
- selection of potentially relevant material;
- analysis of material; selection of specific material;
- incorporation of material into the essay writing process, perhaps in the form of an *argument*.

A further potential 'source' of information lies within the text of a retrieved piece of literature and this echoes our finding in the case study, ie, students' identification of specific sections of text as 'information'. Identifying the specific statements in a text, which capture the essence of the author's perspective, is a key act of learning and development of the student's disciplinary understanding. From a lecturer's position such acts of understanding represented, or not, in a student's essay provide key focal points for feedback and summative assessment of learning.

Our study thus opens up a number of interesting issues concerning this particular group of students' perceptions of information literacy, of their learning task and of their own capabilities as they go about studying. Our focus will now turn in the next three chapters to some of the issues raised by the student interviews, such as epistemological thinking, metacognition and critical thinking, as essential elements of a high standard of information literacy. We explore these issues in greater depth in the next three chapters.

SECTION B

Psychological Insights

CHAPTER 3

Critical Thinking and Information Literacy

3.1 CRITICAL THINKING

As a prelude to the substantive content of this chapter, consider the following concrete example of a set of information literacy activities. Imagine a student who is faced with the task of writing an essay. If we begin to 'unpack' the information literacy activities that this task requires, we immediately see the relevance of critical thinking (which we define and discuss further below). The first task of all for the student is to interpret what the question is asking him or her to do; is it seeking, for example, a description of a phenomenon or theory, is it asking for a much more in-depth evaluation of a theory, or is it asking for competing theories to be compared and contrasted? The answer to that very first question may not be immediately obvious and may require thought and critical reflection. Having interpreted the question, the next step is to identify relevant literature (and note that what is relevant is constrained by the assumed interpretation of the question). There are (at least) three possible answers to the question of where relevant literature containing applicable information comes from: the reading list provided by the lecturer, a broader swathe of reading beyond the reading list, as found by the student, and material identified within texts found by the student. Already, therefore, we have highlighted some important and malleable characteristics of (critical) thinking about an essay such as:

- reading the question/clarifying the topic;
- the disposition to go beyond prescribed reading lists;
- the ability to search for relevant literature independently;
- preconceptions about the topic and essay writing, which influence reading/selection of literature;
- the capacity to make sound judgements;
- the capacity to plan and implement a writing strategy designed to present a suitable (eg, critical) response to the question;
- the disposition and ability to respond to feedback and critical commentary on one's work.

Copyright © 2016 A. Anderson and B. Johnston.
Published by Elsevier Ltd.
All rights reserved.

From Information Literacy to Social Epistemology
ISBN 978-0-08-100545-3

Critical thinking is therefore a broad concept incorporating interpretation of the subject content, interaction of the student with the learning context, the student's reading strategies and information awareness. Taken together, these are perhaps the most immediately obvious key components of critical thinking in relation to information literacy, but as we will see below there are other relevant elements of critical thinking that must be considered.

Before launching into the detailed consideration of critical thinking, we should note that there are *pedagogical implications* of critical thinking and information literacy in terms of course design, teaching, feedback and assessment. For example, it is clear that the teacher's choice of essay topic/question, selection of recommended reading and the nature of discourse in giving feedback and providing assessment are key factors in constructing the wider learning situation represented by the essay task. The lecturer's degree of awareness of information literacy, his/her own capacity for critical thinking, particularly in relation to reflecting on his/her own teaching practice, and his/her capacity to motivate and guide students to good information practice, are therefore central to good pedagogic practice aimed at encouraging critical thinking. We will be exploring the pedagogical implications of what is known about critical thinking both in this chapter and subsequently in Chapter 6.

First, we will explore a number of questions that will help us to clarify the relevance of critical thinking for information literacy. For example: what exactly is meant by the term critical thinking? As we will see, the latter is an umbrella term that is used not only by psychologists but also philosophers and educationalists, and covers a wide range of distinguishably different aspects of thinking. Some elements of critical thinking are particularly pertinent to information literacy and we will focus in particular on these. Having identified some relevant aspects of critical thinking, we will examine (1) the issue of where within information literacy activities these three psychological phenomena manifest themselves, and (2) the issue of how this research literature should best be used to devise better information literacy instruction. In Chapter 4 we will consider how critical thinking relates to epistemology and to metacognition. Note that the literature on critical thinking extensively refers to 'critical thinking skills', and we have already (see the Preface) noted the theoretical tensions between the conceptualisation of psychological activities as skills as opposed to situated activities. We reiterate the view that the 'situated activity' perspective is more nuanced and preferable to the simple notion of a 'skill', since skills tend to be conceptualised as collections of independent capabilities that can be discussed in isolation from each other and from the contexts in which they manifest themselves. We believe that both their independence from each other and from the influence of the context cannot simply be assumed. Where the notion of a skill is helpful, on the other hand, is in implicating the importance of practice at the activity for improving it. Since the literature extensively uses the word 'skill' in connection with critical thinking, we will in reviewing the relevant literature use that term, but the reader should bear in mind that our perspective is rather more elaborated than that, and that 'skill' is being used simply as a convenient shorthand.

The phrase 'critical thinking' encompasses a wide variety of patterns of thinking (eg, Brookfield, 1987; Ennis, 1987; Kuhn, 1991). Ennis (1987), for example, listed some 120 identifiably separate thinking skills that could all reasonably be called 'critical thinking', including, for example, identifying assumptions, identifying and dealing with equivocation, making value judgements, analysing arguments, asking and answering questions of clarification and/or challenge, judging the credibility of a source and so on. Scriven and Paul (2008) provide a useful overall definition of critical thinking: 'Critical thinking is the intellectually disciplined process of actively and skilfully conceptualising, applying, analysing, synthesising and/or evaluating information gathered from, or generated by, observation, experience, reflection, reasoning or communication, as a guide to belief and action'. As Mulnix (2012) notes, whilst there is a learned, skill-like aspect to critical thinking, it is more than the mere possession and exercise of skills: it is not just the blind following of a set of 'rules for good thinking', but a habit of thinking in which the thinker is disposed to use these skills and to accept the results of using them. This implies a degree of metacognitive awareness on the part of the thinker, a point to which we will return below.

A person who is capable of, and in the habit of such thinking is able to evaluate the quality of information he or she encounters to help with decisions about which elements of the information should be accepted and believed, as opposed to mistrusted and ignored. The relevance of such a conceptualisation of critical thinking to information literacy cannot be overstated: at every stage of the process, from initial formulation of an information need through to the final selection of information for attention and use, critical thinking is undoubtedly implicated. Critical consideration of the aim and scope of the information-seeking process would surely help focus the search process on relevant and promising areas; critical consideration of (for example) the selection of keywords and the choice of databases in an online search would again limit appropriately the scope of the results obtained; and critical consideration of the materials obtained in the search according to relevant criteria (eg, peer-reviewed journals in an academic literature search or selection of favourite magazine or newspaper sources for a hobby-related search) would surely help the individual obtain what are for him or her the most satisfactory results.

Taking a broad perspective, it is possible to conceptualise much of the information that we encounter on a day-to-day basis as attempts at persuasive communication. Advertisements and political manifestos are very obviously attempts at persuasion, but arguably academic papers, television documentaries and many if not most of the pages on the world-wide web are also attempts at persuasive communication designed to get their reader or viewer to accept or agree with a point of view or theory, or to believe that some product or idea is worthy of their investment. Given the prevalence of such information sources/persuasive communications, the ability to critically analyse what one is presented with is one that has very general relevance. An ability to engage in critical thinking is therefore likely to not only raise students' academic attainment, but also to enhance their ability to be effective employees and responsible citizens (eg, Perkins, 1989). Conversely, a poor grasp of these skills would clearly imply a poor quality of everyday thinking and problem-solving, and a degree of credulousness, among other difficulties.

Given the wide variety of components of critical thinking noted above, it is useful to try to simplify this plethora of thinking skills. One way of doing this is to conceptualise the core of critical thinking as a type of reasoned argument, and a number of authors have done exactly that (Billig, 1987; Kuhn, 1991; Mulnix, 2012; Perkins, Allen, & Hafner, 1983). Dealing with arguments and the logical relations between them ('the ability to grasp inferential connections between statements', as Mulnix, 2012, puts it) is at the heart of individuals' formulations of their beliefs, judgements and conclusions (Kuhn, 1991), attitudes and categorisations (Billig, 1987) and scientific thinking (Newton, Driver, & Osborne, 1999). For example, Newton et al. argue that argumentative reasoning is central to the practice of science: the scientist must be able to articulate reasons and evidence that justifies particular views, to challenge particular views, to envisage views alternative to their own and to co-construct understanding in collaboration with colleagues. Therefore, it is possible to claim that argumentative reasoning is at the very heart of critical thinking, and that a focus on people's skills at argumentative reasoning and on means of improving these skills would be an excellent way of investigating and improving critical thinking.

Adopting this perspective on critical thinking and following Kuhn (1991), we take 'argumentative reasoning' to include a number of abilities:

1. being able to differentiate opinions from evidence, so that the reasoner does not, for example, simply restate the relevant opinion when asked for evidence in support of it;
2. being able to support opinions with non-spurious evidence, that is, to have a good sense of the quality of different types of evidence and to select particularly compelling forms of evidence in support of one's ideas, rather than unconvincing forms;
3. being able to envision opinions alternative to one's own and to know what evidence would support these,
4. being able to provide evidence that simultaneously supports one's own opinions while rebutting alternatives and
5. being able to take an epistemological stance which involves weighing the pros and cons (by reference to relevant epistemological criteria) of what is currently known.

From the perspective of those who employ university graduates, it is undoubtedly the case that the above set of behaviours is highly valued and a desired outcome of education (eg, see Harvey, Moon, Geall, & Bower, 1997).

A great deal of research has been conducted into the nature of argumentative reasoning, and on how such skills might be improved (eg, Anderson, Howe, Soden, Halliday, & Low, 2001; Kuhn, 1991; Kuhn, Shaw, & Felton, 1997; Perkins, 1989). Much of the research on this topic that has accumulated in recent years appears to imply that the quality of argumentative reasoning in the adult population is typically surprisingly poor (eg, Kuhn, 1991; Perkins et al., 1983). Consequently, an eminently practical concern is how to encourage learners to engage in these behaviours in a more systematic, searching and thorough fashion. We will first of all review some representative studies among the research on argumentative reasoning, present some critique of those studies and then go on to review intervention studies that have attempted to improve the quality of argumentative reasoning.

3.2 THE QUALITY OF ARGUMENTATIVE REASONING

Two early strands of research that appeared to suggest that argumentative reasoning skills in the adult population are somewhat weak are those conducted by Kuhn (1991) and Perkins et al. (1983). Both studies involved asking participants to reason about everyday matters on which they could reasonably be expected to have had a prior opinion, and to analyse their responses from an argumentative reasoning perspective. Kuhn (1991) interviewed adults from a variety of educational backgrounds (for example, some with university education and others with community college education) and asked them to explain the causes of each of three social phenomena (school failure, unemployment and recidivists' return to crime; it was anticipated that the school failure issue would be most familiar to participants, unemployment of intermediate familiarity and recidivism the least familiar). Participants were interviewed individually and asked to say what they thought caused the phenomenon in question, to justify their causal belief ('why do you think X'), to articulate any alternative causal mechanisms that they could envisage ('what do you think someone who disagreed with you might say was the cause of X'), to provide any justifications they could envisage for those alternative 'theories', and to indicate how they would rebut evidence in favour of theories they did not personally subscribe to. Kuhn found that the participants were willing to assert causal explanations, but often confused their 'theory' (Kuhn's term for the participants' causal explanations) with its supporting evidence, for example, by simply restating the theory when asked to provide evidence in support of it. They also frequently generated what Kuhn called 'pseudoevidence', which took the form of richly elaborated plausible scenarios that restated the theory rather than provided genuine evidence for it. Participants also frequently showed a poor ability to envisage alternative theories or evidence in their favour. Expertise in a relevant area made no difference to the quality of argument. For example, parole officers did not reason any better about the topic of recidivism than did other participants. However, Kuhn did find that a college-level education was associated with better performance in that degree-educated participants were better at generating evidence, envisioning alternative lines of causation, and having a more sophisticated evaluative epistemology than participants who had had no further education. However, the performance of even degree-educated students showed room for improvement. Kuhn tested a small number of participants who had expertise in philosophy, and this particular subgroup of participants exhibited the best overall performance.

Perkins et al. (1983) conducted a study which in many ways was similar to that of Kuhn (1991). Perkins et al. presented a written task in which participants considered issues such as whether passing a law to require drinks manufacturers to provide a 5-cent return on empty bottles and cans would reduce litter, or whether the reintroduction of military conscription would increase America's influence in the world. Participants were asked to reflect on the relevant issue for a few minutes, then, having decided what their position was regarding the issue, to set out a case for this position in writing. Their written responses were subsequently analysed for the quality of argumentative reasoning displayed. The results showed that participants often exhibited what Perkins et al. called 'myside bias', which was defined in terms of the numbers of arguments advanced in support of their preferred case as compared to the numbers of arguments advanced for its opposite. In other words, they were prone to engaging in one-sided argumentation, which presented arguments in favour of their own case and neglected possible counterarguments.

Perkins et al. also reported that the arguments provided by participants were flawed in various ways, for example, by failing to anticipate and effectively rebut obvious counterarguments. For example, if arguing in favour of military conscription by claiming that a larger set of armed forces would intimidate potential adversaries, they might neglect to anticipate or rebut the counterargument that, given that modern weapons of mass destruction can wipe out large numbers of troops, the sheer number of troops within an army is a less relevant consideration in weighing up possible influence than it would have done at previous points in history. Perkins et al. suggest that their participants build a mental model of the situation when considering the topic, and they examine this model for robustness. Perkins et al. contrasted two different patterns of critical thinking that they claimed were evident within their data when participants undertook this process of mental model examination. The weaker form of critical thinking was associated with what they described as a 'makes-sense epistemology'. This is the tendency to minimise cognitive complexity by using the simple criterion of whether a given proposition makes intuitive sense and rings true, without critically analysing their mental model very deeply at all. The stronger form of critical thinking on the other hand was associated with a 'critical epistemology' in which participants understood what the potential pitfalls of justification are, and were accordingly more likely to critically analyse their own views by asking themselves when and why their mental model of the topic might fail, and building a model that was more robust against potential objections and criticisms as a result. Interestingly, Perkins et al. claim that whilst the makes-sense epistemology is quite prevalent across their participants, a critical epistemology ought in principle to be teachable.

Both Kuhn and Perkins explain their participants' apparently unimpressive argumentative reasoning performances with reference to difficulties in metacognition. Kuhn's way of expressing this is to assert that participants think with their theories (ie, opinions) and evidence, rather than about them. As a result they have difficulty in coordinating opinions and evidence appropriately.

Kuhn's and Perkins et al.'s work might appear to provide a somewhat bleak picture of the ordinary person's argumentative reasoning skills. The educational implications of such a bleak picture would be profound, because, as we argued above, the patterns of thinking under investigation here are absolutely central to effective cognitive functioning. However, there are a number of methodological and theoretical issues in relation to this research that need to be considered before the findings can be accepted as being generally true.

On the methodological side, it is possible that particular features of the tasks set and of the testing situation might influence the participants' performance. For example, the topics about which participants had to reason were chosen by the experimenter and may have been ones about which the participants knew very little, or had not given much prior thought to. In that connection, a subsequent study by Perkins (1989) is relevant. Perkins (1989) compared participants' reasoning about a vexed personal decision that they had recently been pondering (eg, which university to attend, whether to get engaged), and which they might reasonably be expected to have given some prior thought to and in addition to have cared about, given the dilemma's personal relevance. On the vexed personal issue, their performance was rather less biased and one-sided than was the case with a standard experimenter-supplied reasoning task.

Another possible reason for believing that the seemingly poor performance of ordinary adults in argumentative reasoning tasks might not be quite as bad as Kuhn and Perkins imply is the issue of participants' motivation. In short, are participants unable to reason cogently, or is it the case that they are in fact capable but do not habitually do so? One of Perkins's (1989) studies arguably shed light on this issue. The study involved 'scaffolding' the participants by having a reasoning expert working alongside them on a one-to-one basis. The reasoning expert did not supply content in the form of additional arguments, but instead prompted participants to think more deeply about arguments that they themselves had come up with. For example, the experts requested the participants to rank order the reasons they had thought of in terms of their quality, asked them to think of obvious counterarguments to specific propositions, and in general to reason more thoroughly and deeply. This scaffolding was applied particularly in relation to arguments on the non-preferred side of the argument (the 'otherside'). The result was a striking

(700%) improvement in numbers of otherside arguments provided. There are two possible explanations for this result. The first is that whilst participants often do not spontaneously engage in good-quality argumentative reasoning, it is within their reach (within the Vygotskyan 'Zone of Proximal Development' or ZPD; Vygotsky, 1978). This implies that a training intervention could help effect improvement. The second, more motivationally focused interpretation, is that participants are able to reason cogently if supported (or pushed), but normally decline to do so. There is evidence for both of the above interpretations: Anderson et al. (2001), Kuhn et al. (1997), and Perkins (1989), have found that training interventions do indeed effect improvement. See Anderson and Soden (2002) for a review of some teaching interventions based on peer interaction that have demonstrated improvements in aspects of critical thinking. More recently, Abrami et al. (2012) and Behar-Horenstein and Liu (2011) have reviewed literature examining the effectiveness of teaching interventions in improving critical thinking more generally; this research is considered in a little more detail below. The second, motivational interpretation of the Kuhn–Perkins data alluded to above also fits with much other research (eg, Baron, 1994; Reason, 1990) suggesting that people are 'reluctantly rational', ie, that sound reasoning is effortful and participants are often insufficiently thorough in a variety of thinking tasks. There are, therefore, good reasons for being cautious about any conclusion to the effect that an apparently poor level of performance reflects some sort of stable, enduring cognitive weakness.

A more theoretical set of issues connected with the Kuhn–Perkins work concerns the very nature of the skills involved. Both authors discuss critical thinking/argumentative reasoning as a skill that can, like all skills, be improved with practice. However, doubts have been expressed as to whether the very term 'skill' is an appropriate one to use in connection with argumentative reasoning. For example, Schwartz, Neuman, Gil, and Ilya (2002) distinguish two perspectives on argumentative reasoning. The first is the traditional generic skill perspective (exemplified by the work of Ennis (1987)). This conceptualises critical thinking/argumentative reasoning as a set of general strategies of argumentation that are developed through the life span, that can be deployed flexibly in a variety of contexts, and that can be improved with practice in much the same way that one's playing a sport or a musical instrument can improve simply by doing the relevant activity more often. The second is an activity perspective, which regards thinking and argument as social practices that are exercised and shared within a community, and that are evoked by particular tasks and contexts, rather than skills possessed by individuals and that reside solely at the individual level (Cole, 1996; Resnick & Nelson-LeGall, 1997; Rogoff, 1998). Argumentative reasoning performance is thus conceptualised as an individual propensity that can be used in a variety of situations (ie, is 'domain-general', to use the jargon) within a skill-based account, and as a contextualised activity (where the tools available to participants, the social interactions that occur, the previous history of those involved in the interaction and their goals all exert influences on the quality of the participants' argumentative reasoning performance) in the more domain-specific activity perspective.

The domain-generality versus specificity issue is of considerable practical importance. If argumentative reasoning were in fact domain-specific, as McPeck (1981) suggests is true for critical thinking in general, then argumentative reasoning will be closely tied to the epistemology of particular domains, a point argued also by Willingham (2007). There would, therefore, be '...no reason to believe that a person who thinks critically in one area will be able to in another' (McPeck, 1981, p. 7). This would lead to pessimism about whether it would be possible to teach argumentative reasoning capabilities that would generalise beyond the academic discipline with which they were associated. A strong domain-specific view of argumentative reasoning would also imply that attempting to test this type of thinking by asking participants to reason about general social topics that they may know little about in the way that both Kuhn and Perkins did would produce meaningless results. Kuhn (1991) tackles the domain-specificity issue directly by arguing that argumentative reasoning occupies an intermediate location on the domain-specificity versus domain-generality dimension. In a later paper, Kuhn (1993) claims that her research identified forms of thinking that were domain-general in that they transcended the particular content in which they were expressed. Means and Voss (1996), provide evidence suggesting that there exists a domain-general component to argumentative reasoning.

Recent reviews of the literature (eg, Lai, 2011; Mulnix, 2012) confirm that the above summary of the literature is an accurate one. Mulnix (2012) argues that the case for an argumentative reasoning perspective on critical thinking is indeed a strong one, and that critical thinking encompasses both domain-specific (eg, the standards of evidence quality within a particular domain) and domain-general (eg, the ability to grasp evidential relations) elements. Lai (2011) reviews literature across psychological, philosophical and educational strands of work noting the various possible positions as regards domain-specificity summarised above, and summarising some of the literature on improving critical thinking; this is discussed further below.

Why should argumentative reasoning in particular be relevant to information literacy, as opposed to other more general elements of critical thinking? Certainly it is obvious that such critical thinking activities as judging the credibility of a source of information are (or perhaps we should say, *should be*) of vital importance in information literacy activities. It is also reasonably obvious why argumentative reasoning should be relevant to information literacy activities in an academic context: arguably, argumentative reasoning is quite simply at the heart of all academic work, regardless of discipline. Academic work consists largely of formulating well-constructed arguments supported by discipline-appropriate evidence (and of course, generating that evidence in the first place in the form of research activities). The case for adopting an argumentative reasoning perspective on information literacy activities within an academic context is, therefore, easy to make. But, for example, for more casual information literacy activities such as ones related to hobbies, for example, why should argumentative reasoning matter? The answer to this, we suggest, lies in part with our claim above that much of the information that we encounter on a day-to-day basis can be conceived of as a form of persuasive communication concerning what to believe, or buy, or do in the service of better health, beauty or wellbeing, or who to vote for, and so on. The critical deconstruction of such communications is important in making decisions about which ones we allow ourselves to be influenced by. Those emanating from sources for whom the argument is clearly self-serving, or within which there are logical non-sequiturs or contentious claims, we would do well to be cautious about and it is every bit as important, we would argue, to be able to do this in relation to 'everyday' information as it is in relation to more 'technical' information within academic contexts (See Chapter 9).

Having (we hope) convinced the reader of the relevance of critical thinking and in particular argumentative reasoning to information literacy, the question then arises as to how we can improve the quality of critical thinking, an issue to which we now turn.

3.3 PEDAGOGY AND CRITICAL THINKING: ATTEMPTS TO IMPROVE THE QUALITY OF CRITICAL THINKING VIA TEACHING INTERVENTIONS

There have been a large number of studies that have explored ways of improving aspects of critical thinking, and we will accordingly review a sample of studies that could be argued to have positive implications for how critical thinking can be improved via instruction within an information literacy context. We will consider both general reviews of the literature on teaching critical thinking (eg, Abrami et al., 2008; Behar-Horenstein & Niu, 2011; Lai, 2011; Ten Dam & Volman, 2004) and also more specific studies (eg, Anderson et al., 2001; Kuhn et al., 1997; Schwarz, Neuman, Gil, & Ilya, 2003) to illustrate specific points.

Behar-Horenstein and Niu (2011) review 42 empirical studies involving attempts to teach critical thinking within a postsecondary context. Following Ennis (1989) they distinguish three different instructional approaches: the general approach in which critical thinking is taught as a generic standalone course without reference to specific subject matter, the infusion approach, in which critical thinking is taught within the context of a particular subject matter area but with explicit attention to critical thinking within the subject area teaching, and an immersion approach in which critical thinking is taught within the context of a particular subject matter area but without explicit attention to critical thinking within the subject area teaching. They concluded that greater success resulted when the teaching of critical thinking was explicit rather than implicit, and that treatments that lasted longer tended to result in greater degrees of success than treatments that were shorter in duration. These conclusions fit with the notion of critical thinking as a skill (the literature on skill learning demonstrating clearly that repeated practice of a skill helps enhance it, hence the relevance of the time dimension). They also fit with the notion that metacognition is a key element of critical thinking – those courses with an explicit emphasis on critical thinking being more likely to foster metacognitive monitoring of thought processes. The finding that explicit treatment of critical thinking during instruction yields better outcomes than implicit treatment of critical thinking is supported by findings from Marin and Halpern (2011) and the outcome of the meta-analysis by Abrami et al. (2008) discussed further below. Mulnix (2012) also notes the importance of repeated practice for the promotion of both skill enhancement and metacognition.

Abrami et al. (2008) conducted a meta-analytic review of 117 experimental studies that sought to enhance critical thinking. Across all of the studies reviewed, there was a significant gain in critical thinking as a function of instruction, with stronger gains when critical thinking was associated with explicit teaching objectives compared to when it was associated with implicit teaching objectives. Better results were also found when the teachers or instructors had had special advanced training in preparation for teaching critical thinking skills. They also noted that collaboration among students while developing their critical thinking skills is advantageous.

Abrami et al.'s review provides positive evidence that critical thinking can indeed be improved by teaching interventions.

Ten Dam and Volman (2004) undertook a qualitative review of 55 studies examining the effectiveness of instructional formats for improving critical thinking. They conclude that the characteristics of instruction that are assumed to enhance critical thinking are: 'paying attention to the development of the epistemological beliefs of students; promoting active learning; a problem-based curriculum; stimulating interaction between students; and learning on the basis of real-life situations' (p. 359). They conceptualise critical thinking as the acquisition of the competence to participate critically in the communities and social practices of which the learner is a member, thus acknowledging a domain-specific element and adopting a social constructivist perspective on critical thinking.

As noted above, meta-analyses and reviews of the literature repeatedly emphasise the importance of students interacting together, preferably on meaningful tasks. Examples of studies that have attempted to enhance the quality of argumentative reasoning using peer interaction as a teaching and learning method include those by Anderson et al. (2001), Kuhn et al. (1997), and Schwarz et al. (2003). Approaches using peer interaction and learner–learner discussion are often justified with reference to Piaget's theory of development (see the section in Chapter 5 on social constructivism). Additionally, Crook (1998) suggests two other possible mechanisms that might underpin the benefits that can be obtained from collaborative working. First, during discussion collaborators have to articulate their thoughts publicly, which forces the clarification of the nascent thoughts (see also Palincsar, 1998), and renders them available for exploration. Second, collaborators may co-construct a single, systematising object of thought (such as a hypothesis or a prediction). Accordingly, a number of investigators have applied peer interaction-based teaching methods to argumentative reasoning skills (Anderson et al., 2001; Kuhn et al., 1997; Schwartz et al., 2002). The Kuhn et al. study involved repeated discussion with different partners of the topic of the effectiveness of capital punishment as a deterrent to murder, whilst the Anderson et al. study involved explicit instruction in evidence-based justification with specific reference to proposed project work, followed by discussions of the design of the students' own projects. All three of the studies cited above demonstrated that repeated engagement in peer discussion on a topic results in improved argumentative reasoning (eg, with greater provision of two-sided and comparative arguments and greater awareness of the coexistence of multiple views in the Kuhn et al. study, and better use of evidence-based justification in the Anderson et al. study as a function of having participated in the peer-based teaching intervention).

To summarise, argumentative reasoning skills can fairly be claimed to be at the heart of critical thinking: the ability to infer the relations among arguments with a particular focus upon evidence and justification is central to critical thinking. As noted above, there are reasons for believing that argumentative reasoning capabilities are central to a wide variety of information literacy situations. Whilst there is debate regarding the issue of whether critical thinking skills are generic and apply across situations or are instead domain-specific and therefore tied to particular academic disciplines, there is evidence that good critical thinking has both general and specific elements and that argumentative reasoning skills constitute a generic set of critical thinking skills. It can also be concluded that one strong implication of a skills perspective on critical thinking, namely that argumentative reasoning can be improved as a function of practice, has received empirical support. Improvements in such skills have been more strongly demonstrated when explicit attention is paid to critical thinking alongside subject matter material, when meaningful problem-based learning tasks are employed, when learners interact with each other over their tasks, and when instruction is spread over a prolonged teaching intervention lasting for weeks rather than 'one-shot' instructional sessions. There is here a striking implication for information literacy education. Given the centrality of critical thinking/argumentative reasoning for information literacy, and given the unsatisfactory results from single-session 'one-shot' teaching interventions in improving the effectiveness of critical thinking, it follows that single-session, one-shot teaching interventions will be highly likely to be unsatisfactory for teaching information literacy. This in turn implies that information literacy education would benefit from a curriculum that does not simply list a set of desirable characteristics to be inculcated, but one that embodies an extended temporal progression of activities (possibly extending throughout the undergraduate's entire degree programme) that permits and facilitates repeated, guided practice in relevant information literacy activities that develop and build in complexity and sophistication over time, in much the same way perhaps that research methods teaching typically takes place within a variety of disciplines (See Chapters 5 and 6).

The distinction between a library/digital-skills-based notion of information literacy and wider conceptions of social and epistemological development has implications for how we should teach information literacy, and these implications sit well with our comments above about the desirability of having an extended temporal progression of activities in teaching information literacy. There is currently widespread agreement that the 'one-shot slot' approach is unsatisfactory for all but the most narrowly described teaching and learning. That said, there will obviously be a place for short introductions to more complex designs, or to top up knowledge and skills with new material. However, it is clear from the Johnston and Webber definition (see page 8), and the various elaborated listings of information literacy capabilities such as the ACRL Standards, end the UNESCO statement on Media and Information literacy, that more complex pedagogical designs are required. How might we proceed?

One option could be to adopt a 'short-course' approach. For example, this could map the various elements of an iterative searching process onto an existing course template. The following seven elements could be mapped onto seven sessions: acknowledge information need; identify sources; devise search strategies; conduct search; evaluate results; refine search and repeat as required; apply final results to the perceived need. Sessions would vary in length, mode and design of activities, depending on the constraints and opportunities of a given context. For example a first-year university class conducted in attendance mode might deploy the sessions as part of a lecture sequence spread over 7 weeks. This could take the form of seven workshop sessions, possibly backed by tutorial discussion. Lectures on information literacy could be offered outwith subject study timetables or be incorporated as part of subject teaching. Assessments and examination of attainment could be added either as a separate feature or as part of the assessment of subject learning. Evidently a different concept of teaching would alter the design options and could result in a course, which did not use lectures at all. For example, a problem-based learning approach using projects, team activities and so forth would be an obvious alternative scenario.

In a workplace context, the seven sessions could be designed as a 1-week training course aligned to the specific requirements of a given staff group. Equally the seven sessions could be condensed from 7 days to say 3.5 or 4 days, depending on the needs of the given workplace. Moving from the idea of attendance mode, one could readily envisage an online version being created. A seven-session MOOC is quite feasible and could be made widely available free to the adult learner communities. Allied to both the academic and workplace scenarios sketched here, would be the need for appropriate staff development for lecturers and librarians, to complement their disciplinary and professional expertise. There might also be a need for such provision for learning technologists engaged in designing an information literacy MOOC. One could, therefore, envisage a need to create some workshops to address the staff development requirement.

Arguably it will be much easier to create a sequence of sessions based on a process model of information literacy, than to design a course aimed at engaging learners with more holistic and nuanced accounts. For example, the notion of developing information literacy as '…leading to wise and ethical use of information in society', is perhaps a more complex pedagogical and organisational development challenge. We suggest that our themes of critical thinking and social epistemology are central to devising appropriate pedagogical designs to meet such holistic conceptualisations of information literacy and to enhance the skilled performance of information literacy over time. (We will discuss the issue of course design in more detail in Chapter 6.)

3.4 CONCLUSIONS

Returning to the example with which we opened this chapter, consider again the lecturer setting an essay for a student. We noted earlier that both critical thinking and information literacy are (ideally) intimately bound up in the initial setting of the question and provision of the reading list by the lecturer, the interpretation of the question and writing of the essay by the student, and the final assessment and grading of the resulting essay by the lecturer. What is the contribution of librarians to this extended process? Whilst the lecturer's pedagogical practice for information literacy can be supplemented by contributions from librarians, the main responsibility for initiating information literacy education resides with the lecturer. Discharging that responsibility goes beyond the individual teaching practice of that particular lecturer to include collaborative pedagogical decisions on the nature of curriculum and the design of particular modules and classes within degree programmes.

That said, at any point in the essay experience the student can go adrift – for example, through insufficient motivation; failure to understand the question; inadequate search skills; misunderstanding of the intellectual 'content' of a given source and so on. Staying on track is perhaps effected by a combination of guidance and training by lecturers, librarians, study advisors and peers. To that end mechanisms of advice, guidance and feedback need to be put in place so that student efforts can be supported. However it may be that the key characteristic which needs to be developed by the student over time is *metacognition* – that is, the conscious, deliberate monitoring and regulation of one's own thought processes. We turn to an exploration of that area of psychological literature in the next chapter.

CHAPTER 4

Epistemological Thinking, Metacognition and Their Relation to Critical Thinking and Information Literacy

4.1 INTRODUCTION

This chapter and the previous chapter explore a set of very closely interrelated ideas: epistemological thinking and critical thinking are intimately interlinked with each other. However, each has associated with it a substantial body of research literature that demands a reasonable depth of coverage, and so we have had to split the material across the two chapters. The previous chapter reviewed research on critical thinking and in particular on argumentative reasoning. Such reasoning interacts with the individual's ideas about the nature of knowledge (ie, his or her epistemological thinking). The body of research on epistemological development concerns the way that people's ideas about the nature of knowledge change as they grow up, and also the way that students' ideas about knowledge change as they go through their course, epistemology being the branch of philosophy that deals with the nature of knowledge. The notion of critical thinking (covered in the previous chapter) is clearly closely related to epistemological thinking: *in order to critically evaluate an idea, one must be able to evaluate its strength or weakness as an item of knowledge*, and that in turn presupposes a degree of epistemological sophistication. There is therefore a clear link to information literacy: to be fully information literate, one has to be able to exercise reasoned judgements about the quality of sources, and this in turn requires epistemological thinking to inform such judgements of quality.

Additionally, critical thinking/argumentative reasoning is dependent on the individual's metacognitive skills, that is, the thinker's ability to think about and regulate his or her own thought processes. Again this type of thinking is fundamental to critical thinking, which requires the thinker to be even-handed and unbiased, thorough and fair, and that in turn requires close metacognitive control of one's own thought processes. In the case of

Copyright © 2016 A. Anderson and B. Johnston.

Published by Elsevier Ltd.
ISBN 978-0-08-100545-3
All rights reserved.

both epistemological thinking and metacognition, there is a degree of development that occurs naturally whilst a child grows up, but in both cases the development of the most sophisticated levels of these types of thinking is far from inevitable and there is an extensive literature concerning how to achieve greater sophistication in both epistemological thinking and metacognition across the general population.

This chapter will therefore review research on:

- epistemological thinking
- metacognition

and their interrelationships with each other, which will set the scene for drawing out pedagogical implications in subsequent chapters. All three of these notions are important to information literacy, which is after all not merely a search process but one that requires evaluative decisions about which items among the number retrieved are suitable for the required purposes, and this evaluative and selective process requires all three of the psychological capabilities discussed thus far to be thoroughly developed and fully engaged.

4.2 THE DEVELOPMENT OF EPISTEMOLOGICAL THINKING

There is a growing research literature on the subject of epistemological development, both from early childhood through to adulthood (eg, Kuhn, Cheney & Weinstock, 2000) and also how a university education is associated with epistemological change within undergraduate students (eg, Hofer, 2004). Epistemology concerns the individual's lay 'theory' about the nature of knowledge and what can be known. Kuhn and Dean (2004) summarise the development of epistemological ideas through childhood as follows. The youngest children take a realist view of knowledge in which beliefs have a direct correspondence with external reality; knowledge originates from external sources, and is certain. Such a view of knowledge implies that critical thinking would be completely unnecessary, since external reality simply provides us with true beliefs and there is nothing to be questioned, as observed in our own case study (see Chapter 2) and the study by Whitmire (2003). Slightly later (from about age 4 onwards) the child becomes aware of the possibility of people holding false beliefs. The knower is now implicated in the generation of knowledge, but the knowledge is regarded as being either correct or incorrect in a very clear, absolute way. This categorical approach to knowledge is known as the absolutist level; an absolutist epistemology does imply acceptance that critical thinking has relevance, and that its role is to compare assertions to reality in order to determine their truth or falsehood. Later still (with the onset of adolescence) a multiplist epistemology emerges in which all opinions are equally valid (as expressed succinctly in the adolescent mantra, 'whatever'). A multiplist epistemology would envision critical thinking as irrelevant, since all opinions on a subject are equally good and there is no point in trying to select among them – 'everyone has a right to their opinion'. Finally, the most sophisticated type of epistemology recognises that opinions are not all equally good in that they can be supported by evidence (or not), which in turn can be of high quality (or not) – this is the evaluativist position in which critical thinking serves the function of evaluating and selecting among competing views on the basis of their degree of support by evidence. Kuhn and Dean (2004) note that absolutist and multiplist views are common in adults, and indeed a fully evaluativist epistemology tends to be associated with having undergone tertiary-level education. The implications for information literacy if Kuhn is correct about the relative prevalence of the different types of epistemological thinking within the population are clear: only a proportion of the most highly educated subgroups of the population will perceive the need, and routinely be in the habit of, exercising critical thinking in relation to information obtained from whatever source. The risk is that for a substantial proportion of the population little or no critical thinking is brought to bear on information, either because it is simply assumed to be correct, or because it is only one of potentially many equally valid competing items. In that context it is perhaps easy to see why so many people seem to view information literacy as solely about the processes of searching for information; it might simply not occur to them that critical evaluation is desirable or even possible, depending on their level of epistemological development. Such a view of the population as a whole and of the relatively sparse prevalence of sophisticated epistemological thinking and its attendant processes of critical thinking is somewhat bleak, and would imply that substantial educational efforts would be required to realise UNESCO's slightly idealistic vision of fully information-literate populations (see Chapter 8). However, we should note here that the essentially pessimistic view of Kuhn is not universally shared (eg, Freire (2006) and Mezirow (1978; see Chapter 6) take an altogether more optimistic stance as regards people's capability to change their way of seeing things and to adopt an altogether more critical perspective). Additionally, Kuhn herself (eg, Kuhn, Shaw, & Felton, 1997) has shown that peer interaction can be an effective vehicle for improving critical thinking. There are, therefore, justifications for pursuing the goal of improving critical thinking even if some assessments of the critical capabilities of the general population suggest that they are somewhat less than strong.

Research on epistemological development in undergraduate students started with the work of Perry (1970) who interviewed a sample of male undergraduates at different time points throughout their degree studies. He noted a general trend such that students during the course of their undergraduate studies changed from a relatively primitive, unsophisticated (absolutist) epistemology through various possible intermediate stages to an ultimately more sophisticated (evaluativist) epistemology, although there was no guarantee that a student would reach the highest levels of epistemological sophistication by the time they graduated, and indeed some graduate students show evidence of not having attained the highest levels in this progression.

Thus, in their beginning year students tended to subscribe to a view of knowledge which was absolutist and 'dualist' – that is, knowledge was perceived as having definite correct or incorrect content. Furthermore, such students' epistemology was also 'realist', ie, it held that knowledge content that is correct has a direct correspondence with real entities and states of affairs in the world. Such a student might regard the atomic theory of matter as correct and true, and would therefore believe that matter really *is* made up of tiny particles as described by atomic theory. As students moved further on within their courses, they began to take a less dualist and realist stance. So, for example, at one of the intermediate stages in Perry's nine-stage scheme of epistemological development derived from this research, students acknowledge that a variety of views might exist on a given subject and that all are equally valid, ie, the 'multiplist' view noted by Kuhn and Dean (2004). At the late stages of their undergraduate career, the students are more likely to exhibit more sophisticated types of epistemology, the most advanced of which is a fully evaluativist view of knowledge. This holds that the 'reality' of many issues is ultimately unknowable. The existence, for example, of subatomic particles is inferred from particle collisions and examination of the apparent behaviour of fragments, rather than direct observation of those particles. Knowledge and theory are therefore inevitably tentative and subject to revision or replacement in the light of new data. A further corollary is that the convincingness of a theory is dependent on the quality of the evidence that supports it. This epistemological position requires the student to be comfortable with ambiguity and uncertainty, and to be willing to radically change his or her mind should new evidence overturn a previously dominant theory in favour of a newer one; it has to be acknowledged here that our own case study, and other similar work such as that by Whitmire (2003) and Jones and Allen (2012) suggest that fully evaluativist thinking of this kind is relatively rare, at least in the junior years of the undergraduate programme. Hofer and Sinatra (2010) claim that maturation alone does not prompt epistemological development; there is therefore no guarantee that older individuals such as adult returners to university study would initially show high levels of epistemological sophistication and we could therefore expect them to initially subscribe to a dualist and realist, or possibly a multiplist epistemology in much the same way as we would expect school-leaver students to do. Indeed our own case study data (see Chapter 2) suggest that this is the case.

Following Perry's seminal work, a number of different theoretical approaches to the issue of epistemological thinking have been developed. The interested reader is recommended to consult Hofer (2001b, 2004) for more detailed reviews of the variety of theories of epistemological thinking and the variety of approaches that have been adopted towards measuring epistemological thinking. However, it is worth noting in passing that a variety of views on the nature of epistemological thinking exist within the literature, and that these different views have implications for how such thinking should be measured and how it might be improved by teaching. Perry's work (and that of some other theorists such as King & Kitchener, 1994; Kuhn, 1991) presupposes a *developmental* change in which epistemological thinking develops through a succession of stages from relatively unsophisticated through to more sophisticated, as outlined above. Such approaches typically involve investigating epistemological beliefs via interviews.

A second approach (eg, Schommer, 1990) characterises epistemology as a collection of *beliefs* about knowing that may be more or less independent of each other rather than developing in a coordinated sequence. Such beliefs are a trait-like aspect of the individual. This approach typically involves measuring epistemological beliefs using paper-and-pencil questionnaires involving rating scales. A third approach has been to conceptualise ideas about knowledge and knowing as being organised into coherent *theories* (eg, Hofer & Pintrich, 1997). If the beliefs postulated by the 'belief' theorists are coordinated and integrated, the result could become much more theory-like, which makes it difficult to clearly separate out the belief and the theory positions from each other. A final approach theorises that epistemological knowledge exists as a set of *resources* which are more fine-grained and less general than beliefs or theories, and these resources get called into play in particular educational contexts (eg, Hammer & Elby, 2002). This approach has a useful emphasis on how particular strands of epistemological thinking might be called into play by particular classroom tasks and contexts. It would be fair to point out, though, that the 'resources' theory is less well developed and has less of a research base currently supporting it than the developmental and the belief/theory approaches.

The two dominant approaches among those reviewed above, therefore, are the developmental approach and the belief/theory approach. The developmental approach implies that educational interventions intended to change the learner's current epistemological level should be couched just above that level rather than greatly above it, in line with Vygotsky's (1978) well-known idea of the zone of proximal development; exposure to ideas that are well beyond the learner's current reach could be confusing and counterproductive. This leads to teaching strategies involving challenges originating from the next most sophisticated level of epistemological thinking that are designed to foster epistemic doubt. These challenges come from a number of sources. One, for example, would be encouraging student comments and questions, since within any given classroom there will be some degree of variation across learners in their current level of epistemological thinking and as a result whole-class discussions that are carefully managed by the teacher can capitalise on this variation to help learners move to the next level of sophistication. (We note in passing that once again – see also Chapter 3, and the discussion of social constructivism below – that structured peer interaction is seen as an important potential vehicle for effective pedagogy.) A similar approach would involve adoption of a learner-centred approach in which groups of students discuss ill-structured problems and are encouraged to gather and evaluate data and reflect on their assumptions about knowledge, with encouragement and support from the tutor.

The belief theory also has implications for the effect of education in changing epistemological beliefs. Hofer (2001b) argues that the fundamental epistemological assumptions that underlie critical thinking could be identified and prioritised for teaching. For example, the assumption that not all problems have a single correct answer; that science progresses and some ideas are discarded and replaced by new ones; and that what initially appear to be diametrically opposed theories can sometimes be synthesised into a single new framework could all be prioritised in the design of teaching and learning.

Two final complications about epistemological thinking are worthy of note here. The first concerns whether epistemologies are tied to particular areas of learning (ie, are 'domain-specific'), or instead rather more general in scope ('domain-general'). This distinction, as we saw in the previous chapter, is also prominent in research on critical thinking. If epistemology is domain-specific this opens up the possibility that a given individual might show epistemological sophistication in the specific domain in which he or she has been trained but less sophistication in other domains. Thus, for example, a psychologist might be acutely aware of the uncertainties surrounding knowledge within psychology but regard knowledge in other areas of science as much more certain and secure. Were epistemological thinking to turn out to be domain-specific, this would point to a need to link instruction to specific academic subjects and contexts. The implication for information literacy instruction would be that it should be tied closely to the particular academic discipline that the student is majoring in, rather than being taught in an abstract or context-free way.

The second complication concerns the teacher's or instructor's theory of epistemology and the influence it may have on the teaching and learning experiences that he/she devises. If the teacher or lecturer subscribes to a dualist/realist epistemology it is entirely possible that in both the learning experiences that he/she creates for students, and in the modelling of information-literacy-related thinking that he/she provides, the students will be encouraged to think about their discipline and the information that relates to it in a dualist/realist way. This would tend to discourage (either actively or by default) the kind of critical thinking that we argue is an essential part of a full information literacy capability.

Another useful aspect of belief theory is that, given that the beliefs can be measured by questionnaires, the results can be related to other constructs such as strategy use and cognitive processing. In particular, it can be linked to the idea of metacognition which we discuss below.

To summarise, there are a number of different views within the psychology literature as regards epistemological thinking – whether it exists as a set of linked beliefs, whether it characteristically displays a predictable developmental progression, whether it is tied to specific domains of knowledge and so on. The broad consensus appears to be that there are a variety of positions that can be taken regarding the nature of knowledge. Some hold that knowledge can simply be correct or incorrect; from an information literacy point of view, the individual's task would simply be to identify ways of accessing the 'correct' knowledge. Others within the population hold that a variety of views can co-exist and be equally valid (the 'multiplist' position), and the implication from an information literacy point of view would be that it would be difficult or impossible for them to choose between competing sources of obtained knowledge. A fully relativist/evaluativist view of knowledge would hold that there are no absolutely right or wrong answers on many topics, but some potential answers have more evidential support and should be regarded as more credible than the others. It is really only for this last epistemological position that critical thinking as a tool for selecting among information sources becomes a meaningful concept. Such critical thinking processes should ideally be fair, balanced and thorough, and to ensure that that is the case, careful control of the thought process by the thinker him/herself is implicated. This is the area of metacognition, to which we now turn.

4.3 METACOGNITION

The term metacognition literally means 'cognition about cognition', or the ability to think about and to regulate one's own knowledge and mental processes. This area of research originated in the work of the developmental psychologist Flavell (1976, 1979), which initially focused on metamemory, ie, our understanding of our own memory processes. The idea of metacognition was subsequently taken up by a number of other researchers and its scope broadened to include, for example, the planning, monitoring and evaluating of one's own learning processes (eg, Tanner, 2012) and what might be termed social or shared metacognition, that is, the joint regulation of cognitive activities by groups of learners during classroom tasks (eg, Garrison & Akyol, 2015). Many authors draw a distinction within metacognition between awareness and regulation of the content of thought (metaknowledge), and of one's strategies for tackling problems (metastrategy). This distinction parallels the well-known philosophical distinction between declarative (knowing that) and procedural (knowing how) knowledge. Kuhn and Dean (2004) note that 'metacognitive skills typically do not develop to the level we would like' (p. 270) and discuss some possible ways of enhancing metacognition. Ideally, during the course of development metacognition should become more explicit and effective as the individual develops an increasing degree of conscious control over his or her own thought processes.

Development is typically not characterised by sudden transitions in the quality of thinking such that at one stage thinking uniformly operates at one level and at the next stage, thinking uniformly operates at a more sophisticated level. Instead, it is the case that at any given stage a variety of, eg, strategies are in operation but the overall balance determines the individual's current developmental level. Developmental change is therefore a shift in the frequency of usage of strategies such that, whereas previously less sophisticated strategies were predominant, more sophisticated strategies have come to predominate. How to encourage this switch in the overall balance of strategy usage, pedagogically speaking, has been the subject of much discussion and research. Kuhn (2000) argues that a good approach to encourage metacognitive development is to provide practice at a social (groupwork) level the cognitive forms that we wish to see operate at the individual level. A process of interiorisation as theorised by the developmental theorists Piaget and Vygotsky (see the next chapter on constructivism and learning) results in the originally socially realised process subsequently being used by the individual when acting alone.

Research conducted by Christine Howe et al. (eg, Howe, Rodgers & Tolmie, 1990; Howe, Tolmie, & Rodgers, 1992) demonstrates that childrens' performance can be improved markedly by appropriate instruction. These researchers have demonstrated that even complex skills such as how to test a scientific hypothesis validly can be improved using an instructional technique called 'scaffolding'. This instructional technique was first used by Wood, Bruner, and Ross (1976), and involves a careful use of 'contingent prompting', that is, prompting that is contingent upon whether the child's action in the task is successful or not. The original Wood et al. study involved mothers helping their toddlers to complete a task involving the construction of a wooden pyramid from a collection of interlocking parts. The task was carefully designed so that at any given stage, only one unique piece was the correct one to use, and that this would be readily perceivable by the adult. Wood et al. noticed that the mother–child dyads who were most successful at this task (in terms of solving the problem rapidly) interacted in a particular way, such that if the child performed part of the task successfully, such as, selecting the correct piece of the puzzle that will build the next part of the pyramid, the prompting by the adult was deliberately kept rather vague. If the child made an error, the prompting by the adult became more specific, and increasingly specific with each successive error until it got to the point where the adult demonstrated the required action. Subsequent successful action by the child resulted in the prompting becoming less specific again. Howe et al.'s research involved the use of similar contingent prompting, but the task this time required the children, who worked in groups, to learn how to test hypotheses about the optics of shadows. Contingent prompting was shown to be helpful to the (late primary school age) pupils' ability to generate a sound hypothesis, and furthermore, the performance increase included generalisation to novel problems. Thus, the childrens' metacognition about how to go about testing hypotheses improved, and this improvement generalised to new problems.

It should be added that similar improvements in learning conceptual knowledge in physics using structured peer interaction was demonstrated in undergraduate students (Howe, Tolmie, Anderson, & MacKenzie, 1992), and similarly, the preparation of designs for undergraduate dissertations within psychology was improved using a computer-supported peer-interaction-based task (Anderson et al., 2001). Likewise, Anderson, Howe, Soden, Halliday and Low (2001) demonstrated beneficial effects of structured peer interaction on further education college students' critical thinking skills. It is clear therefore that appropriately structured peer interaction tasks can be used to improve not only conceptual learning and hypothesis testing by primary school children, but also both concept and skill learning within groups of adult learners. Extending this kind of approach to the learning of information literacy (both its conceptual and its more skill-based elements) is a step that we intend to explore in practical terms more fully in the future, but we offer some suggestions based on this previous research below.

Tanner (2012) published an interesting paper on how to promote metacognition within biology teaching. Her focus was on how to explicitly teach metacognitive strategies to learners, and on how to create a classroom culture grounded in metacognitive strategies. She used a well-known distinction within the literature among three aspects of metacognition, namely metacognition about planning, monitoring and evaluating, to generate a series of questions that teachers could encourage students to ask themselves during classes, when doing homework, in relation to exams, and in relation to the overall course. Tanner suggests that these questions could either be shared directly with students, or embedded into particular assignments to encourage a metacognitive level of thinking about the learning process. For example, students might be asked during the last 5 minutes of a class to note down on a card their answer to the question, 'what was most confusing to me about the material explored in class today?' This encourages reflection on what was presented, identifies specific areas or points that the student can subsequently address during private study, and if used regularly in class creates a climate in which it is accepted that a degree of confusion is the norm when confronted with new material, and is something to be resolved rather than an insurmountable barrier or a symptom of deficiency on the part of the student. Another suggestion by Tanner that has resonance elsewhere within the literature that we have reviewed (eg, the material on teaching critical thinking reviewed in the previous chapter) concerns the modelling of metacognitive thought processes by the teacher. This can be done by showing explicitly how she, as a teacher of biology, thinks procedurally in solving a problem – how to start addressing the problem, how to decide what to tackle first and subsequently, how to check the work as it proceeds and how to know when the work is satisfactorily completed. This kind of modelling could be used in any disciplinary context. This type of work is a good example of the kind of pedagogical changes that led ACRL (2015) to revise its framework. Table 1 of Tanner's paper bears a striking resemblance to Secker and Coonan's (2013) framing and also fits well with the ACRL (2015) revisions; this will be explored further in Chapter 6.

Tanner's three areas for metacognitive development – planning, monitoring and evaluating – map rather neatly onto equivalent terms used to describe different phases of online searching. This strongly suggests that Tanner's work on metacognitive prompting for each of these three phases via appropriate questioning could readily be translated into information literacy teaching contexts. The interested reader is directed to Tanner (2012, p. 115) for fuller details of the range of metacognitive prompts that she recommends, but we have adapted some of her metacognition-prompting questions below, and added one or two of our own, for use in an information literacy search task. We would envisage a class of students being divided into groups of two or three in a computer lab, and being tasked with jointly undertaking an information search task that is meaningful to them (ie, is part of their normal subject curriculum and serves a genuine purpose such as identifying relevant literature for a forthcoming assignment). This group work could be enhanced using Tanner's metacognitive prompting.

For example, metacognitive prompting at the planning phase of a search task might include questions like:

- What is the instructor's goal in having me do this search task?
- What are all the things I need to do to successfully accomplish this search task?
- If I have done something like this before, how could I do it better this time?

To capitalise on the possibilities for learning afforded by peer interaction, the above questions could initially be considered and answered individually, and the answers compared and discussed. Differences and discrepancies are likely to spark fresh ideas. For the same reason, we suggest that actual execution of the search task and evaluation of the results could profitably be undertaken in a group (two- or three-person) setting to maximise the exchange of ideas and to prompt further insights via discussion.

Metacognitive prompting at the monitoring phase might include questions like:

- What strategies are we using that are working well, or not working well in the task?
- What is most challenging for us about this task? What is most confusing?
- How could we change our strategy to address these challenges and confusions?

Metacognitive prompting at the evaluation phase might include questions like:

- To what extent did we accomplish the goals of the task?
- How would the instructor evaluate our performance in the task?
- In future, in what ways would we do this task differently?
- What have we learned about searching as a result of taking part in this exercise?

A final useful part to the proceedings would be to have the instructor chair a whole-class plenary discussion in which the students could air their search strategies, keywords used and other techniques deployed. In that fashion all class members could learn from each other, and indeed from the instructor's approach if he/she had undertaken a search and was to share the details of his/her strategies and approaches to the task.

It is thus relatively straightforward to create teaching and learning exercises for information literacy learning that capitalise on Tanner's metacognitive prompting and long-established research on peer interaction. Note that we envisage a number of such exercises within the students' curriculum over a long time period, guided by a vision of a curriculum which has clearly defined and carefully sequenced aims and objectives, both in terms of particular skills or techniques that are to be acquired, and also in terms of conceptual content.

The link between metacognition and critical thinking was explored in a study by Ku and Ho (2010). This small-scale study compared five students who had been identified as better at critical thinking according to their scores on the Halpern's Critical Thinking Assessment Test Using Everyday Scenarios (see Halpern, 2007) with another group of five students who had performed less well on this test, in terms of their metacognitive planning, monitoring and evaluating when solving five critical thinking tasks. The students spoke as they went about solving the tasks (ie, generated so-called think-aloud protocols) which were coded in terms of the sophistication of their planning, monitoring and evaluating processes. It was found (despite the small numbers of participants involved) that the 'high' critical thinking group produced significantly more high-level planning strategies (such as planning specific steps – eg, 'I should read this paragraph one more time before I do anything') and significantly more high-level evaluating strategies (eg, 'I think what I just said only answers the question partially, it needs to be further elaborated') than the 'low' critical thinking group. Examples of the low group's planning and evaluating strategies were 'what should I do next?' and 'my answer may be too brief', respectively, which are less specific than for the 'high' group. The result for monitoring was in the predicted direction but was not statistically significant. The study thus suggests that, as we might anticipate, better-quality critical thinking is associated with more elaborated metacognitive processes.

This study by Ku and Ho links up to our case study finding, that students can conceive of 'information' as being 'in' a text. This is rather different from the idea of searching a database for information, which might be associated with librarian/lecturer concepts of information/information literacy. There is also an interesting reflection here of the question – 'how/when do I know I've got enough information for my purposes?', which comes up in learning situations. For example: 'This paragraph in the textbook is enough because it has some relevant sounding words and of course it's in a recommended textbook'; and also in areas such as health care, eg, 'Do I settle for what the doctor tells me, or do I Google my symptoms for more information?', and political decision making, eg, 'Should I decide my vote based on this party leaflet or seek out the full manifesto, or indeed go to a public hustings meeting and ask questions?' These are all significant examples: if the student only accesses a bit of a textbook, they may well underperform or fail; a patient who accepts the doctor's opinion at face value may lose the capacity to discuss the doctor's statements; the voter who settles for a relatively simplistic policy statement in a leaflet may not grasp the detail of the policy or the problems, which might emerge in critical debate.

4.4 EPISTEMIC METACOGNITION

One application of epistemological and metacognitive research to information-literacy-relevant problems was reported by Hofer (2004). In her study, students were asked to think aloud whilst in the process of conducting online searches for a simulated class assignment (not necessarily in their own 'home' discipline) in an effort to explore the students' epistemological processes as they went about their task. Retrospective interviewing after the tasks were completed was also used. Hofer does not provide detail on how many students were involved in this study, or what levels of study within their degree programme they were engaged in at the time of the study. She does, however, report some general observations on their performance.

She reports that students did make comments during their think-aloud online searches that indicated that they were metacognitively monitoring the epistemic quality of what they were accessing and making epistemic judgements on what they were finding. Hofer noted similar phenomena to those we discussed in our own study: if students view knowledge as simple and certain, then, for example, having found research literature that appears to establish a specific point, there is less motivation to find either contemporary or more recent evidence that qualifies or even contradicts that evidence. Indeed, one way to deal with such complexity is to ignore it, and Hofer reports some evidence of students adopting precisely this strategy. Increasing expertise (as measured by courses or classes taken) results in greater willingness to seek out recent information in case thinking has changed within the relevant area, although students were somewhat hazy about how they might establish that a particular article had been peer-reviewed, even if they were aware that peer-reviewed articles were preferable. There was also evidence of a degree of domain-specificity, with some differentiation being made among search engines when searching in their 'home' discipline but reversion to more general searching techniques, such as Google, when searching in a less familiar discipline. Overall, for most students, search processes are not especially thoughtful or deliberate even though epistemological considerations sometimes did explicitly surface, and their selection of material and decisions to discontinue searching were made rapidly and not always thoughtfully. These findings are therefore consistent with earlier findings from our own study and from that by Jones and Allen (2012) discussed in Chapter 2, and suggest a number of loci where teaching and learning interventions could usefully be created and used.

4.5 CONCLUSIONS

The psychological literature on epistemological thinking and on metacognition are, we argue, highly relevant to information literacy education. Both of these phenomena underpin critical thinking, and the success of the latter (or indeed whether it manifests itself on a particular occasion at all) depends on the individual's level of epistemological thinking and also on his/her metacognitive control. Fortunately there is now substantial evidence that the right sort of teaching and learning experience involving structured peer interaction with metacognitive prompting can, if practised over a period of time, help students develop better performance in these areas.

CHAPTER 5

Student Learning and Information Literacy

5.1 INTRODUCTION

The previous three chapters have explored various aspects of student thinking. Here we link these to the students' approach to learning and study skills, and consider their implications for pedagogy. The currently accepted broad theory of learning within both school and adult learning contexts is known as constructivism; here we consider constructivism in relation to pedagogy, transformational learning and information literacy (IL).

5.2 CONSTRUCTIVISM

The dominant theory for explaining the phenomena of pupil and student learning at the present time is known as constructivism. It can usefully be contrasted with what one might describe as a 'lay' theory of teaching and learning, which is widely held among the public, and is often referred to as the *transmission* view. In the latter view, learners initially start as the proverbial 'empty vessels' and the teacher's role is to contrive the right sorts of messages concerning the content of the lesson, so that the learner readily understands that content. If the teacher gets this right, the knowledge, as it were, flows smoothly and seamlessly from teacher to learner. 'Good' teaching therefore involves successful communication on the part of the teacher, who has the sole responsibility for making this transmission process succeed. Simple-minded as it is, it is not difficult to find, for example, pronouncements by politicians on educational matters that strongly presuppose this simple transmission view.

The theory of constructivism takes a quite different view of the teaching and learning process. The essential point is that rather than conceptualising the situation as one in which teachers present knowledge to learners who have to learn that knowledge and move from a state of 'no knowledge' to 'some knowledge', constructivism asserts that learners *construct knowledge for themselves*, and the teacher's job is to arrange learning

Copyright © 2016 A. Anderson and B. Johnston.
Published by Elsevier Ltd.
All rights reserved.
From Information Literacy to Social Epistemology
ISBN 978-0-08-100545-3

experiences to help learners with this construction process. The presumption is that even very young children actively try to make sense of their world, and in consequence arrive at primary school with a considerable amount of knowledge (albeit not always 'correct' according to received academic wisdom) already in place. Indeed, there is a substantial literature on children's intuitive ideas, for example, about physics, biology and economics – see Sara Meadows's book *The Child as Thinker* (2006) for an overview. See Box 5.1 on intuitive physics for an example of such phenomena. For adults, of course, it is even more likely that their previous experiences will have led them to develop intuitive ideas about the topic under consideration (whether that be physics, biology, psychology – or even information literacy), and these intuitive ideas may or may not be helpful. According to constructivism, therefore, the learner is an active rather than a passive participant and the teaching and learning process is more of a dialogue than a monologue transmission.

The upshot of the constructivist conceptualisation of learning is twofold. First, learners are rarely if ever completely 'empty vessels' when beginning to learn a topic, and in some cases these intuitively arrived at ideas, that are both counterproductive from the point of view of getting learners to understand accepted theory in an area, and the ideas themselves can also be highly resistant to change. Second, the teacher's role is as an arranger of experiences that challenge a student's prior conceptions, and to help the student learn new and possibly counterintuitive content. As Alison King (1993) so eloquently expressed it, the teacher is no longer 'the sage on the stage' but a 'guide on the side'.

The theory of constructivism stems from two main sources: the theories of the developmental psychologists Jean Piaget and Lev Vygotsky (see Meadows, 2006, for an accessible introduction). Piaget emphasised the importance for learning of conceptual conflict, that is, conflict between current knowledge and belief on the one hand and new information on the other. There are two main sources of conceptual conflict. One is an experience that the individual undergoes – as for example, when the results of an experiment in a school physics lab contradict one's expectations (eg, the object that one has just confidently predicted will float in water has just sunk) and an explanation is called for to explain the discrepancy. Piaget's theory emphasised that ultimately the individual has to be able to assimilate the new information, and if necessary this might require him or her to change (accommodate) the previous ways of thinking to make this possible. Presentation of conceptual challenge followed

Box 5.1 Intuitive Physics as an Example of Learner Preconceptions

Since the early 1980s researchers have demonstrated repeatedly that learners who are new to physics come to the subject with pre-existing prior conceptions concerning how the physical world works. Take for example Newtonian mechanics, that body of physics that deals with force and the motion of objects. As children grow up and interact with the physical world (for example, playing ball games), they formulate intuitive ideas about how the physical world works – what patterns of motion will result from various ways of kicking or throwing a ball, for example, plus intuitive ideas about concepts like momentum. These ideas however can conflict with accepted physical theory. Take a simple example: the behaviour of a dry ice 'puck' when a force is applied to it. The puck is a small container like a jar lid, and it is placed on the bench inverted so that the empty space it contains is adjacent to the bench. Under this puck is placed some solid carbon dioxide ('dry ice'). This gas has the unusual property that it sublimates, in other words it goes straight from solid to gaseous form as its temperature rises. The solid form is only stable at a temperature below −78.5°C at atmospheric pressure, and when the dry ice is exposed to normal room temperature it sublimates to form a 'cushion' of gas under the puck, which is then free of friction with the bench on which it formerly rested, rather like a miniature hovercraft, and it can be used as a (temporarily) frictionless body for experiments. The question is: how do you get it to move at a constant speed? An air hose is available to apply either a brief blast of air or a continuous one. Which type of force (instantaneous or continuous) should be used?

Newtonian theory states that if no force is acting on a body, it is either at rest (a claim that most people find to be quite uncontroversial) or moving at a constant speed in a straight line (a claim that many learners find highly counterintuitive). It is rare to encounter truly frictionless conditions; we are used to having to keep pedalling a bicycle, for example, to keep moving because otherwise friction from the road surface and wind resistance will slow us down and eventually stop us. The answer to the problem is that with a truly frictionless body like the dry ice puck, an instantaneous force will set it moving at uniform speed in a straight line, whereas a continuous force will cause it to accelerate. When learners are tasked with setting it moving at a steady speed, because their preconceptions are formed in the real world where friction and air resistance routinely operate, they will often apply a continuous rather than an instantaneous force and are surprised to see the puck accelerate. This simple example of preconceptions contradicting received theory demonstrates the sometimes unhelpful effect of prior conceptions. Teaching cannot assume that the learner has no prior knowledge, and indeed teaching may have to begin by making explicit and subsequently challenging a prior conception that the learner is likely to hold. There is evidence that if problems are sufficiently difficult, even quite sophisticated learners who

Continued

BOX 5.1 Intuitive Physics as an Example of Learner Preconceptions—cont'd

are studying physics at university level will revert to these prior conceptions. Should there be any equivalent of prior conceptions in the area of information literacy, they could have a similarly negative impact on learning the relevant concepts and skills.

The idea that learners will have prior conceptions concerning situations in which information has to be used is quite a plausible one. For example, learners may make any or all of the following assumptions (and these may be more or less justified, depending on the context):

- Too much or alternatively too little information relevant to their purposes will be available;
- All or most of the relevant information will be provided by teachers/ authorities;
- Searching or researching for information is seen as a 'step' in another process needed to achieve a particular outcome, rather than as a phenomenon in its own right that is worthy of explicit attention and reflection;
- The relevant information will be mainly obtained by reading, listening, talking, and asking questions;
- Decisions about the relevance and/or quality of information are mainly made on an intuitive basis or determined by task-related criteria.

All of these prior assumptions could potentially affect the way in which the learner goes about his or her information searches on any particular occasion, but they would also affect the way the learner responds to more general instruction in information literacy.

by individual reflection (possibly structured or guided in some way by the teacher) would be a pedagogy that flowed naturally from Piaget's ideas.

Another source of conceptual conflict is when other people articulate ideas that are different from one's own, and some attempt is made to resolve the discrepant view. Vygotsky emphasised this more social type of conceptual conflict, although Piaget and those researchers who followed in his footsteps (see, eg, Doise & Mugny, 1984) also emphasised the importance of peer interaction as a source of conceptual conflict. The pedagogy that would follow from this would be one that involved structured peer interaction, and a number of researchers have developed structured peer interaction tasks and demonstrated that these are effective in helping learners learn new conceptual content (see Box 5.2).

BOX 5.2 Constructivist Pedagogy in Practice: Peer Interaction and Learning

A considerable body of evidence has now accumulated that broadly supports the constructivist theorists' view that peer interaction can be conducive to learning. These studies typically adopt an experimental approach in which individual learners are pretested to assess their knowledge on the topic under investigation. Following this, they are set to work in pairs or small groups on tasks that require them to firstly articulate their views to each other, test predictions and explain any discrepancies between predictions and outcome, and then subsequently they are individually post-tested to assess any change in their knowledge of the topic. The pre-to post-test differences in scores for the experimental (peer interaction) group are then compared to a control group or those from a previous cohort to ensure that it is the peer interaction-based teaching intervention rather than simply the passing of time and the accumulation of knowledge from other teaching sessions that is proving to be effective.

For example, Howe, Rodgers and Tolmie (1990) examined the effect of peer interaction on primary school children's understanding of the physics of floating and sinking. The development of ideas on why particular objects will float or sink in water typically goes through a fairly regular progression. The youngest children (eg, under 5 years old) will claim that whether an object floats or sinks is a matter of volition, ie, the object 'wants' to float or sink. Slightly older children will mention relevant variables such as the object's weight, shape, or the type of material from which it is constructed but nevertheless fail to consider these variables in relation to one another. Such considerations are associated with the next stage of sophistication, in which learners explain floating or sinking in terms of object density (ie, weight relative to size and shape), claiming that dense objects will sink and less dense objects will float. This more sophisticated position is also espoused by many adults. However, it is only partially correct. A physicist would explain floating and sinking in terms of *relative* density, that is, the density of the object relative to the density of the medium in which it is placed. Relative density explains why ice floats in water but sinks in whisky: ice is less dense than water but more dense than whisky. Relative density also explains why a coin will sink in water but float in mercury.

Howe et al. pretested the children with questions asking them to predict whether particular objects (eg, a cork, a key and so on) would float or sink in water. This allowed the researchers to ascertain the children's initial state of knowledge about floating and sinking. Subsequently children worked in groups with instructions to compare their individual predictions with each other (to induce conceptual conflict), to come to an agreed joint prediction, to test that prediction by putting the object into a tank of water, and to explain the resulting outcome. The task was therefore carefully designed to make explicit to the

Continued

BOX 5.2 Constructivist Pedagogy in Practice: Peer Interaction and Learning—cont'd

learners the existence of conceptual conflict (in terms of differences among individual children's ideas, and in terms of discrepancies between predictions and observations), which was intended to act as a spur to the learning of more advanced ideas. Children were 'post-tested' on their knowledge a few days later, and again some weeks later. It was found that ideas about floating and sinking had improved only a little at the first post-test, but they had significantly improved when retested some weeks later, long after the task had been completed. This set of findings points to two conclusions: first, inducing conceptual conflict via peer interaction and direct observation is effective in improving the learners' conceptions, and second, this learning may take some time to come into effect, requiring a period of reflection or consolidation for the learning to take place.

This type of work has been replicated in other areas of physics learning such as motion down an incline and free fall under horizontal motion. Clearly, the learning of conceptual material can be improved using peer interaction. Similar experimental studies have demonstrated that the effect extends beyond conceptual learning to the learning of thinking skills – for example, Anderson, Howe, Soden, Halliday and Low (2001) showed that further education students' critical thinking skills could be improved relative to a control group using peer interaction and group discussion. In the previous chapter, we sketched out an equivalent teaching and learning intervention based on peer interaction that should be helpful in inculcating information literacy skills. In essence, structured peer discussion could be used at all phases of the information literacy exercise, from refining the initial information need, through listing possible search terms, to executing the search and making decisions about which of the 'hits' obtained are most suitable for the students' purposes. We suggest that a tutor-led plenary discussion of all phases of the process can also be helpful in reinforcing some of the conceptual aspects of information. A good example of exactly this approach applied to information literacy is reported in a paper by Kuiper, Volman and Terwel (2009), in which primary school age children undertook a web enquiry on healthy eating, and did this search as a collaborative activity. Both domain content knowledge (regarding healthy food) and web literacy skills showed evidence of improvement. The approach that we are advocating is completely compatible with ACRL (2000) Standard one Outcome one, which envisages students engaging in discussions to help identify their information needs (and indeed goes somewhat beyond this to extend the same peer-based approach to subsequent phases of the search process), and Secker and Coonan's (2013) claim that active or enquiry-based learning is vital to the development of information literacy.

5.3 CRITIQUE OF CONSTRUCTIVISM

Although, as noted above, constructivism is a dominant theory of learning and pedagogy at the present time (a point conceded even by critics such as Irzik, 2000; Meyer, 2009), it has not escaped criticism, particularly in relation to science education. Meyer (2009) argues that since constructivism adheres to the view that all knowledge is constructed by the individual, it implies that (1) correspondence between knowledge and objective reality (truth) is no longer relevant, and (2) all items of knowledge constructed by an individual are equally good, making it impossible to distinguish between knowledge and superstition. However, Meyer (by his own admission) is attacking a particularly radical variant of constructivism (Von Glasersfeld, 1995), one that many adherents of constructivism would not subscribe to (Irzik, 2000). Irzik (2000) argues that, on the positive side constructivism has helpfully emphasised the importance of learners' prior knowledge and the importance of active engagement in learning. On the negative side he argues that constructivism confuses knowledge and belief, and the replacement of the notion of truth (as the correspondence of knowledge to an objective reality) with the somewhat more vague notion of 'viability' leads some constructivists to lose the distinction between right and wrong answers (sic) in science education. Furthermore, he argues that 'it is naïve to expect the students to discover all or most of the relevant scientific truths by themselves'. Osborne (2014) notes that some critics of constructivism equate constructivist pedagogy with unguided discovery learning. However, he points out that leading constructivists explicitly acknowledge a need for input from the teacher; in short, equating constructivism with unguided discovery learning is a species of straw man argumentation. Osborne also, however, criticises constructivism on the grounds that, whilst it has usefully drawn attention to the prior knowledge that the learner brings to the learning experience, it does not fully acknowledge the counterintuitive nature of much scientific knowledge, and it does not make stipulations about the selection and sequencing of content, nor how to encourage the development of metacognition in students. Overall, whilst there are some critiques of constructivist ideas within the literature, many of these critiques are made of extreme case or straw man formulations of the constructivist idea, and many advocates of the basic constructivist approach would see it as being fully compatible with realist/objectivist notions of truth and endorse the claim that the role of the teacher is to introduce counterintuitive theoretical notions and to guide the idea construction process in the direction of accepting scientifically accepted notions.

5.4 STUDY SKILLS

Given that a considerable body of research evidence supports the constructivist view of learning, it is now well established as the accepted account of how learning takes place. However, it is pertinent to ask questions about how students typically go about their learning process. What sorts of consolidation and revision activities do they in fact engage in? And how *should* they do this, given the implications of constructivist theory?

The term 'study skills' refers to the conscious and deliberate control over the mechanisms of learning that students use in an effort to retain taught material. There are many books (a good and very well-known example being that by Cottrell, 2008) and websites (for example, a Google search conducted at the time of writing using 'study skills' as a search term yielded some 59 million hits) devoted to study skills and how to use particular techniques such as drawing so-called 'mind maps' effectively. The fact that deliberate conscious control is involved harks back to our discussion of metacognition in Chapter 4; not only should learners be using particular techniques, but they should simultaneously be aware that they are using these techniques and should be critically evaluating how well they are using them and how useful they are proving to be, whilst they are using them. Both particular techniques such as aids to effective reading of text, and also more global/organisational matters such as time management, are implicated within study skills. Thus a typical study skills book or Website will cover such areas as effective reading, writing, notetaking, time management, working with others, engaging in critical thinking and revision. Take the issue of reading text, for example. There are a number of suggested systems for enhancing a learner's approach to reading. One such is SQ3R (Robinson, 1978), which stands for 'survey, question, read, recall and review'. This recommends that learners begin with an initial overview reading ('survey'), then formulate questions about the text (either broad ones concerning how the material within it relates to other topics already known about, or more narrow and specific comprehension questions), then read the text again (searching for specific information, taking notes and re-reading iteratively), then attempting to recall key points from within the text content, and finally reviewing the relation between the recall content and that in the original text.

These study skills are usually meant to be used in the service of what Entwistle (2001) refers to as 'deep' learning. Entwistle was among the first to contrast deep as opposed to surface approaches to learning. Deep approaches are very meaning-focused, pondering the conceptual relations within the material to be learned, and between the learning material and other information already known. Surface approaches to learning involve rote memorisation with the aim of regurgitation of this material at a subsequent examination. These approaches are strategies that are consciously adopted by learners rather than characteristics of the learner, so that a particular individual might adopt a deep approach in relation to a preferred academic subject, but adopt a surface approach to another less preferred subject. The relation to constructivist theory should be fairly obvious: the deep strategy involves consideration of meaning and attempts to construct an inner model of the relations between the meanings of particular concepts, very much in line with constructivist theory. The literature has moved on beyond the initial deep versus surface distinction (see the collection of papers in Entwistle & Tomlinson, 2007). But the fundamental idea of the importance of constructing meaning as key to thorough understanding and long-term retention remains valid. However, it should also be noted that study skills techniques can be used in the service of rote memorisation ('shallow' learning); much depends upon the learner's intentions, which of the many available study skills techniques they choose to use, and on how they ultimately use them.

Assuming that the appropriate pedagogies are in place, and that the students' study skills are adequate or good for the purposes of learning, the outcome should (we hope!) be that the students will learn whatever knowledge and skills their course is attempting to impart. However, it is pertinent to pose the question: what form will that learning take? Will it simply be the accumulation of knowledge about a particular subject matter area, plus some requisite associated skills in a kind of accretion process, or will it have more far-reaching consequences in terms of fundamentally changing the way the learner thinks? Both of these outcomes are possible; the theory of transformative learning emphasises the possibility of education inducing wide-ranging changes to the individual's habits of thinking (see also the discussions in Chapters 2 and 9).

5.5 CONCLUSION: IMPLICATIONS FOR INFORMATION LITERACY INSTRUCTION

We have covered a considerable amount of ground within this chapter. There are however two key sets of messages that we want to extract concerning the processes by which we promote successful learning, and how these processes can be applied to instruction in information literacy. Finally, we examine how the material covered within this chapter relates to our developing model of information literacy.

First however, the key 'take-home' messages are:

Learners construct their own knowledge in an area, with two implications:

They will have intuitively formed prior knowledge before any instruction

The teacher's role is more facilitative and interactive than didactic.

Pedagogies (eg, based around peer interaction) should be designed to encourage the learner to realise that there is a conflict between what they have hitherto believed and what they are experiencing now.

Peer interaction can be an effective vehicle for learning conceptual material and some thinking skills, but improvements in individual learning may unfold over an extended period of time rather than immediately.

Study skills techniques can be used to enhance a learner's understanding and retention of material. They can also however be (mis-) used in the service of rote memorisation without any 'deep' understanding.

There is some evidence (albeit slightly contentious, already touched upon in Chapter 2 but reviewed in more detail in Chapter 9) that courses can result in a type of transformative learning in which the individual's broad patterns of thinking are profoundly altered; ideally this should include much more explicit awareness of information and how to deal with it, and a much more systematic and ordered approach to using it.

A second point that emerges is the importance of context to defining the nature of information and the form of information literacy within that given context. For example:

- Is information in the foreground of a given context?
- Is the educational context framed as constructivist or transmittal? That is, is the rest of the course taught in a constructivist or transmission-based way? This would help establish an ethos which in turn would influence the learner's response to IL instruction.
- Is the purpose of obtaining the information in a given context high or low stakes – for example, will it affect a mark that is a key component of a student's final grade, or not?
- Is information seen as mainly textual or mainly verbal/non-verbal?
- Are professional or commercial information systems entailed?
- Are librarians or other mediators involved?

The third point is the necessity to map the relations between formal models of information behaviour such as the Big6 (Eisenberg and Berkowitz, 1990) and constructivism, for example:

- Are there symmetries/asymmetries between such models and constructivism/transmission?
- How do criteria for evaluating information in a given model relate to the constructivist notion of making meaning?
- Is the 'information science' that is embedded in search engines known to users?

An important point in relating information literacy and constructivism in a given educational setting, like a degree course, is the extent to which information literacy is explicitly acknowledged as an active/constructive aspect of teaching and learning, as opposed to a tacit awareness of a need to 'do something' about information. Arguably a tacit awareness is the common default position wherein information is regarded as a secondary contribution to some major phenomenon like 'learning' or 'writing an essay'.

A consequent strategy for improving IL could involve making IL more explicit and valued, perhaps by using IL-specific formal instruction to improve awareness of IL and practical ability in information handling, together with assessment incentives to influence learners. In effect this would mean creating a learning design, which fully acknowledges IL as a body of learning in its own right as opposed to a learning design that treats IL as little more than a need to 'do something' about information, but, for example, relying on learners to have sufficient prior knowledge or to simply 'pick up' IL as they go along.

An important condition here is that instructional librarians typically have had to rely on 'one shot' sessions with students as their primary means of developing IL. This tends to militate against the introduction of more complex and arguably rewarding course designs. Consequently, advocating course design as an important mechanism to deliver constructivist teaching and learning, needs to take the limitations on instructional librarian practice seriously. That said, many librarians are dissatisfied with the constraints of one-shot sessions and are actively seeking opportunities for more complex strategies. A useful approach to this problem could be to provide examples of what more complex learning designs based in constructivist approaches might look like and how they might be introduced to institutional practice.

At this juncture, it is appropriate to revisit the basic model of information literacy that we first set out in Chapter 1, altering it by fleshing out

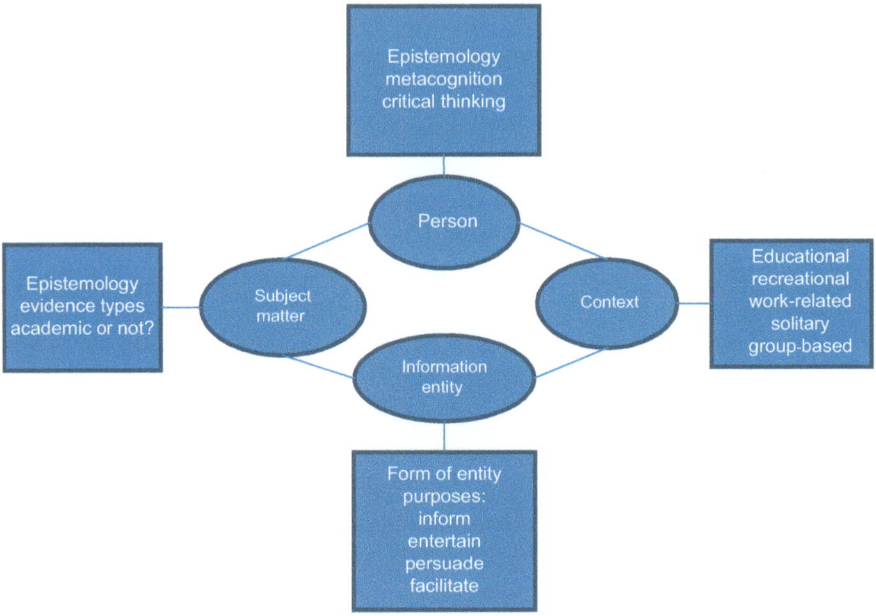

Figure 5.1 The revised version of our model, first discussed in Chapter 1.

some of the psychological properties, varieties of contexts, purposes of information entities and subject matter presuppositions, to yield Fig. 5.1.

The model now begins to flesh out aspects of the Person, Context, Information Entity and Subject Matter nodes, although we do not claim that this fleshing-out is exhaustive. A key focus for us in this and the previous two chapters has been the psychological properties of the person – their (developing and changing) epistemology, the degree of metacognitive control of their thinking and their critical thinking and argumentative reasoning capabilities. Note that the Subject Matter node is also associated with an epistemology, and it may not coincide with the person's epistemology – indeed, it could be argued that a key purpose of any higher education degree programme is to bring the person's epistemology more into concordance with that of the academic subject, on the assumption that the two epistemologies will initially be different from each other.

We have focused within this chapter on educational contexts in which information literacy activities are relevant, given our own role as educators. However, for other contexts (such as recreational and work-related contexts), the same considerations apply: the individual's epistemological thinking, critical thinking and metacognitive skill will influence the course and outcome of an information literacy situation, as when, for example, purchasing or voting decisions are involved.

The nature of the information entity has also been somewhat fleshed out – its form can be quite varied (eg, book, website, software application, television programme or indeed some entity created by the user him/herself such as a written document or photograph, for example). Its purpose can also be quite varied, and the individual's critical approach will vary depending on purpose (eg, if seeking to be informed about some issue, accuracy of the information may be uppermost in the individual's mind, whereas if the individual's purpose for the information entity is to be entertained by it, then the critical faculties might deliberately not be used in a process of 'suspension of disbelief').

In fleshing out the context node, we have included the distinction between solitary and group-based activities. It is something of a cliché to assume that, for example, Internet use is invariably solitary but one key take-home message of this chapter is that appropriately structured group-based activities using the Internet provide an excellent vehicle in which information literacy skills can be learned.

In the next chapter, we look at our last psychological phenomenon, that of transformational learning, and begin to look at curriculum development for information literacy in the light of the psychological phenomena that we have discussed in the book thus far.

SECTION C

Contributions from the Library and Information Sector

CHAPTER 6

Curriculum Development and the New Curriculum for Information Literacy

6.1 INTRODUCTION

This chapter draws together psychological ideas from Chapters 3 to 5 under the theme of curriculum inquiry and development and relates them to a major development in professional thinking and practice – Secker and Coonan's New Curriculum for Information Literacy. A key issue to arise will be the relationship between the curriculum for a given subject discipline, and a curriculum designed from a basis in information literacy (IL).

Our first task is to integrate the various psychological strands described in preceding chapters, and describe them in terms of a theory of adult learning, which is applicable to higher education and which offers insight into the wider field of learning in everyday life. The work of Jack Mezirow (1978, 2000) on transformational learning is helpful in illuminating the adult learning aspect of the university experience. Our second task is to set out an overview of the nature of curriculum inquiry and development in higher education and to consider the practice of course design and re-design as a practical vehicle to introduce psychologically informed pedagogy to learners in a systematic way, which can be incorporated into an institution's academic decision-making processes. We use the work of John Biggs on constructive alignment (1978, 2011) as a means of achieving this aim.

Our third task is to explore the contribution Secker and Coonan's (2013) 'New Curriculum for Information Literacy' might make to enhancing the scale and effectiveness of information literacy education in higher education, thereby helping to solve the curricular problems of where information literacy is to be introduced, in what way and to what extent. Since the New Curriculum material is readily available in print form and online, we will not provide a detailed summary. Instead we will concentrate on discussing how it might be used to channel a psychologically informed account of information literacy in practice and crucially how it might be

From Information Literacy to Social Epistemology
ISBN 978-0-08-100545-3
Copyright © 2016 A. Anderson and B. Johnston.
Published by Elsevier Ltd.
All rights reserved.

used, by interested academics and librarians, as a tool to bring about change in their courses. In essence we will attempt to view the Secker and Coonan curriculum through the eyes of lecturers and, critically, through the eyes of academic decision-makers who have influence over the shaping of faculty-level pedagogical change.

This chapter is in three parts:

- Transformational learning: Dramatic versus incremental transformation
- Curriculum inquiry and development: Course design for transformation
- New Curriculum for Information Literacy: From one-shot slots to continuous educational development.

The three previous chapters have drawn upon psychological literature in a number of areas – particularly epistemological thinking, critical thinking and metacognition, and pedagogical notions about the nature of learning and study that we hope to (1) weave into a coherent whole and (2) use to infer some recommendations for information literacy instruction. It seems clear to us (and we hope that by now we have also convinced the reader) that the quality of an individual's information literacy is going to crucially depend upon both his or her searching skills (a point that is by now quite well explored within the literature) and also his or her critical thinking skills. The latter in turn crucially depends upon the epistemological views held by the individual, and their metacognition: the former will influence what type of criticisms will be made (if any) of found items of information, and the latter will influence how thorough, objective and fair the critical thought process is.

At this point it is perhaps worth pondering what would be the outcome of the rigorous application of a pedagogy that successfully encouraged the development of epistemological thinking, metacognition, critical thinking, search skills and knowledge of information as an abstract concept. The outcome, surely, would be an overall qualitative change in a person's information literacy, not simply in the narrow sense of their then being able to conduct more efficient, rigorous and critical searches to help them find desired information, but in an altogether broader sense of altering their way of thinking about the world of information more generally. *In effect, the person would have been transformed.* This term has come to be used particularly in the field of adult learning: the notion of *transformational learning* (eg, Mezirow & Taylor, 2009) denotes a substantial change in the learner's perception of him/herself and their place in the world. We now turn to a brief explanatory overview of what has grown to be a substantial body of literature.

6.2 TRANSFORMATIONAL LEARNING

The theory of transformative learning was first developed by Mezirow (1978) following a study of American women returning to postsecondary education or the workplace after an extended time away, and has undergone a series of revisions over the years (eg, Mezirow, 2000; Mezirow & Taylor, 2009). This genesis in adult education has particular resonance with our work on adult returners to higher education in Chapter 2. Whilst our case study was clearly defined in terms of a specific pre-entry course it was aimed at a general population of entrants rather than the more familiar school-lever population of most undergraduate education. The case study indicates the fluidity between formal higher education, the workplace, the labour market and the general population, and it is also worth noting that this general population constitutes the majority of citizens and employees in the knowledge economy. We will return to discussion of this population in Chapter 9.

The fundamental idea is that learning has a transformative effect on the learner, so that the learner comes to think differently as a result of having undergone a course of formal education. Mezirow's (1978) adult returners, for example, having completed a college re-entry programme, came to see themselves for the first time as the product of challengeable cultural expectations. The awareness of these hitherto unperceived and therefore unquestioned cultural assumptions concerning women's roles in society results in the forging of a new identity involving greater autonomy, personal control and responsibility for their lives. This perception is somewhat different to a more limited sense of learning outcome, often held at pre-entry and entry level to a course of study, and expressed in terms of acquiring 'new skills and knowledge' whilst obtaining a specific qualification.

Mezirow describes this type of emancipation as an example of *perspective transformation*. A perspective comprises an individual's values, beliefs and assumptions, and constitutes a kind of filter through which personal experience is made sense of. When individuals find they can no longer use their current set of values and beliefs to make sense of an experience, transformative learning can occur to allow the development of a new perspective which is more developed in the sense of being more inclusive, discriminating, open and reflective (Mezirow, 2000). The initial study (Mezirow, 1978) examined women's emancipation from traditional roles and societal expectations of them in a process of consciousness raising, but the idea of transformative learning is quite general and can be applied much more widely to other areas of thinking. For example, degree courses within higher education are often argued (by those who teach them) to be vehicles for encouraging learners to think more systematically and critically in a quite general way. The graduate therefore in a very real sense thinks differently about all sorts of areas compared to the non-graduate. This (assuming it to be the case) would be another example of transformative learning.

Mezirow (1978) in the earliest version of the theory claims that the initial spur to transformative learning is what he calls a 'disorienting dilemma', that is, a dawning awareness that the current perspective held is in some way or ways no longer adequate. This leads to a questioning and critical appraisal of the psychocultural assumptions underpinning the current meaning perspective, resulting in the development of a new, transformed perspective. More recent formulations of the theory (Mezirow and Taylor, 2009; see Kitchenham, 2008, for a summary) argue that transformation occurs at both the more global level of meaning perspectives and also at a lower, more specific level of particular meaning structures. This newer version of the theory therefore distinguishes between meaning schemes (which are narrow and specific constellations of concept, belief, judgement and feeling) and meaning perspectives (which are global overarching structures, each comprising a number of meaning schemes), and both can be subject to transformative learning.

Meaning schemes can be expanded, added to, or transformed, whereas meaning perspectives are transformed following critical self-reflection on the assumptions that supported the perspective. One vehicle that is argued to be effective for promoting this critical reflection and transformation is student dialogues with their peers (Thomas, 2009; Tisdell, 2008). This very much ties in with our discussion above about social constructivism, although the latter focused very much on the learning of much lower-level conceptual material. It is entirely possible that peer interaction could help promote the more global change in perspective that Mezirow discusses.

Although the theory of transformative learning has, historically, been subject to various lines of critique (and some of these criticisms are discussed below), its central tenet of transformative change remains both the cornerstone of the theory and a useful concept for characterising change in adult learners as a function of their educational experience.

A critique from Newman (2012) poses radical questions about transformative learning, asking whether it exists at all, and whether the term transformative learning could simply be replaced by the phrase 'good learning'. He makes a number of critical points about the literature on transformative learning. For example, he asserts that significant change can occur in learners without the radical change implied by the word transformation, even in individuals who complete entire university degrees. He argues that the evidence for transformative learning is usually based on qualitative data and in particular claims from the learners themselves that they have experienced a transformation, and that such affirmations 'have no guaranteed validity' (Newman, 2012, p. 40); ultimately we only have the learner's word for it. He claims that transformative learning differs from other types of learning, if it does at all, by a matter of degree rather than in kind, and that there is therefore nothing particularly distinctive about it. He notes that the experiences that provoke supposed transformative learning can be small-scale and cumulative, rather than dramatic disorienting dilemmas. He argues that some forms of discourse advocated by Mezirow as facilitating transformation (eg, accepting consensus) are not uniformly positive in their effects and neither are they invariably desirable. Finally, he criticises the spiritual emphasis which some authors in the transformative learning area adopt; Newman argues that spirituality is an inherently problematic topic to study.

We would contend that whilst Newman raises some appropriate and valid questions, some of his points are somewhat overstated. For example, transformation learning theorists have already acknowledged that disorienting dilemmas are not necessary to provoke transformation; less dramatic accumulations of smaller-scale events can succeed in provoking transformation (Mezirow, 2009). Likewise, the fact that some researchers choose to discuss issues of spirituality within the framework of transformation learning does not in itself invalidate or fatally undermine the broader framework even if one is sceptical about the academic rigour of the theorising about and investigation of spiritual matters. Newman's scepticism, however, does raise valuable fundamental questions about what is unique about transformation learning, as opposed to other types of learning, how frequently genuine transformative learning occurs within the population, assuming that it does exist at least sometimes, and how best to measure it. Taking the latter point first, Newman is apparently sceptical about qualitative data and relying simply on participants' assertions about transformation (although we note an inconsistency in Newman's position on this issue: he appears (Newman, 2012, p. 41) to be happy to accept the assertions made by Cranton's (2006) participants – ironically citing consensus as a positive reason for doing so, presumably because these are consistent with his thesis that transformative learning does not exist).

Our own position would be that we would not be willing to completely discount participants' assertions, but would certainly be happier if they were to be corroborated by other measures. What would be ideal in this context would be evidence that the thinking, as measured within experiments or by reliable and valid psychometric tests, eg, of university graduates was noticeably different from the thinking patterns of non-graduates, and indeed there have been some studies which suggest that this is the case (Lehman & Nisbett, 1990; Nisbett, Fong, Lehman, & Cheng, 1987), although some (eg, Perkins, 1985) claim that this is not as dramatically different as a transformation learning theorist might imply. Nor do we find it especially troublesome for transformation learning theory that individuals do not invariably claim to have been transformed as a result of completing studies at college or university. For example, the literature on epistemological development (Hofer, 2004; Kuhn, Cheney, & Weinstock, 2000; see also Chapter 4 above) clearly demonstrates that some individuals can graduate university without having attained high levels of epistemological thinking; profound change in thinking patterns is clearly not inevitable, and this implies that there is a strong need to re-design courses and adopt more effective pedagogical strategies in order to achieve more significant transformations. In this connection it is worth recalling the study by Whitmire (2003) of students at an Ivy League University; although this group of students can be assumed to be a particularly able group intellectually, they were in fact not very different in their epistemological thinking compared to our adult returners, as described in Chapter 2.

But Newman's central questions remain: does transformation learning exist, and if so, how frequently does it occur and how does it differ from other forms of learning? One pertinent question to raise in this context is: under what circumstances do people make positive claims about having experienced a transformation? Going back to the original Mezirow (1978) publication, the participants were making retrospective claims about the overall effect on their thinking of college courses in which they had participated. Such reports are therefore global retrospective reflections involving the participants looking back over a reasonably extended timescale. In doing so, they are summarising across what must have been cumulatively a large number of small-scale, concrete learning experiences and attesting to the overall cumulative effect of those experiences on their own thinking. This seems to us to be, on the face of it, a not unreasonable or implausible set of claims on the part of participants. As noted above, more recent statements of the theory of transformational learning acknowledge both global changes in perspective (as discussed in the original statements of the theory; Mezirow, 1978) and smaller, more 'local' transformations of 'meaning schemes' (Mezirow, 2009). It is, perhaps, the latter that particularly lead to difficulties in distinguishing transformation learning from other types of learning.

In short, it seems premature to dismiss entirely the notion of transformational learning, even if there are serious questions about whether the variety of phenomena described and discussed within the literature on transformational learning are or are not instances of the originally envisaged qualitative shift in individuals' thinking. We contend that it is entirely possible that (and indeed there is some evidence to the effect that) a prolonged educational experience such as a university degree considered as a whole can in fact be transformational for the individual undertaking it, even if it is not so in all cases. The intriguing questions then become:

- Why is a given experience like a degree apparently transformational for some individuals but not for others?
- What educational experiences could be built into courses to encourage the kind of qualitative change suggested by transformation learning theorists?

These questions implicate curriculum inquiry, course redesign and pedagogy and demand that we identify those key points in a course of study where interventions are needed and may produce best effects. For example, our first question might be hypothesised in terms of an essentialist notion of learning potential, which accepted that some students are simply 'brighter' than others, and that little can be done to change this. Or a different position might be adopted, which proceeded from the view that whilst individual differences might be i n play, it is equally plausible that a redesign of teaching, learning and assessment practice could even out apparent differences, and lead to an overall improvement in attainment for all.

Our second question about qualitative change above leads us straight into the application of social constructivism to practice, eg, how particular pedagogies, such as structured peer interaction or problem-based learning, could be used to effect positive change in information literacy.

In order to illustrate the issues raised by designing a credit-bearing module on information literacy we use the experiences of one of the authors (Johnston) in developing such a module at the University of Strathclyde in the late 1990s. For a more detailed account see Johnston and Webber (1999, 2003). The course design challenge implicated in the development of the module can be characterised as a mix of institutional requirements, pedagogical opportunity and constraint:

- Requirement to add value to the degree in terms of enriching student learning and contributing to the development of graduate attributes in relation to employability in the form of a credit-bearing elective;
- Opportunity to design a whole, credit-bearing module going beyond basic skills teaching to involve more complex ideas about information literacy;
- Opportunity to apply constructivist strategies to teaching and learning;
- Constraint of 'fitting' the module into the student's overall degree/year of study structure(s).

The module was a third year elective option so all students who took the module were looking at final year projects/dissertations coming up in the following academic year (honours degrees in Scotland take 4 years). Consequently a concept of information literacy in terms of understanding and improving use of sources, searching and analysis of found information was highly relevant. In short, the students could 'apply' the information literacy taught them to the kind of academic situation they were about to be in and gain discipline/task-specific experiences. Some of them were doing the pre-honours practice assignments in year 3, which were becoming a feature of curriculum development in the late 1990s, so they got an instant benefit from our class. Johnston and Webber managed this close match to immediate and near-future situations by designing the assessments to align with the needs of their other classes, so that students could engage with our tasks in the context of the module and in the context of their degree subjects and requirements to develop research and information capacities.

This took us out of the 'bolt on' territory of particular bits of information literacy 'bolted on' to a pre-existing class, and into the territory of disciplinary difference, epistemological development, complex academic tasks and relevance of academic subjects to the job market. We included the students in discussion of what IL might mean beyond skills and how it might relate to the nature of their other subjects and the ways in which they were taught and helped to learn. This was successful and quite illuminating. For example, students were well able to discriminate between different kinds of subjects, eg, 'fact-based' subjects like accountancy and 'thinking-based' subjects like management science. These perceptions were used by the students to explain why the subjects were taught the way they were. Hence it was 'obvious' that accountancy was a largely transmittal experience, due to the factual, right/wrong answer nature of the subjects, whilst management science was much more constructivist given the need to form opinions and develop solutions, often collaboratively, as that was the sort of consultative role that management science graduates often had to do in their careers. (We used Alison King's (1993) 'Sage on the stage, guide on the side' paper to focus the discussions, so the students became familiar with this kind of language.)

As an added dimension, the students reported differences between year of study/approach to study. Thus in first year they 'liked' straightforward lecturing, because once they'd mastered the art of taking notes, they could get on with being first-year students and having a good time. However by third year they recognised that with the imminence of job applications/interviews, they needed to be able to display greater employability. Equally they wanted more interesting and challenging learning by that stage. Consequently constructivist strategies involving projects, teams, presentations, complex problems, sophisticated information use, etc., were much more attractive.

Johnston and Webber (1999, 2003) gathered data from the students and subsequently published their experiences based on 2 years of data-gathering with students. As a guide to enhancing the academic practice of module design and teaching based on this experience, the rubric might be – plan it, do it, research what you are doing and publish it. As this was probably the first example of a credit bearing information literacy elective in the UK it is worth noting.

However, the practice of pedagogical change is not simply a matter of what individual teachers might decide to do in the light of their understanding of social constructivism. In formal study situations the unit of analysis and action is the course of study – modules, years of study, etc. – or more accurately the *design* of the course. The overall nature of the curriculum for a given degree programme is equally important, since this will include requirements from society, the state and the economy to achieve outcomes for employability, ethical behaviour and rising to the opportunities and challenges of the Internet age in addition to discipline-specific content. We will deal more fully with these issues in the following section on the work of Secker and Coonan.

In summary we can present the fundamental concepts of transformational learning in relation to information literacy in the following way:

- *Meaning schemes*: Approaching information literacy as a relatively straightforward set of information skills associated with a particular study task in a given context.
- *Perspective change*: Adopting a more sophisticated and holistic understanding of information literacy, which includes explicit appreciation of one's epistemological beliefs and reflection on their meaning in wider contexts.

Perhaps the key transformation for our purposes might be that of *becoming an information-literate person*. This would involve a shift in one's notions of the *meaning* of information literacy and the adoption of a new higher-level *perspective*, which acknowledged the value of information and its decisive role in society, and not simply within a narrower disciplinary or academic context. An information-literate person in our terms would be one who is consciously engaged in forms of social epistemology.

6.3 CURRICULUM INQUIRY AND PRACTICE: TOOLS FOR TRANSFORMATION

In order to create the conditions for perspective transformation, or any account of learning for that matter, we need conceptual tools, which allow educators to operate at a more systematic level of organisation than simply applying their disciplinarity to student learning, using various teaching 'techniques'. In short we need a vision of a curriculum, which identifies all of the features of a given education and which provides the backdrop to specific manifestations such as degree courses and major component parts such as modules.

We see curriculum as a particular facet of educational research and also as a practical aspect of the organisation of study in schools, colleges and universities. Our perspective on curriculum is holistic and includes: '… content, pedagogy, process, diversity and varied connections to the wider social and economic agendas…' (Johnston, 2010, p. 111/112). In terms of information literacy we are concerned with all of the following: sources, skills and processes, and the broader field of social use of information and knowledge.

Research and practice in curriculum can have multiple entry points:

- subject content;
- student learning;
- pedagogical research, practice and innovation;
- critical thinking and information literacy;
- boundaries between curriculum in formal organisations like universities and the wider socioeconomic context;
- workplace learning;
- informal adult and community learning;
- staff development in pedagogy;
- implementation of digital and other technologies for learning purposes.

The above is often the contingent way that staff go about curriculum change – in a list-like, particulate way. Consequently, a holistic construct is required to avoid fragmentation and isolated development. And yet, the widespread modular structure of courses tends to militate against this, with modules being developed by different individuals in quasi-isolation from each other. A cross-module and indeed cross-year perspective is needed, in much the way as is done, for example, for research methods teaching within social science degrees, for example: module X will contain statistical concepts A, B and C, module Y will contain D, E and F, and in subsequent years. In short the design has to be on a whole-course level and quite possibly integrated with the development of various personal characteristics and employment-related graduate attributes. Information literacy could be approached through this shaping of a given course design.

Both researchers and practitioners need to be able to have a helicopter view and be able to pull together these various strands of learning and information activity into a more unified pattern of relationships. Once patterns have been established they can be used to organise how education is packaged in the form of both a descriptive prospectus and also a plan for educational activity in the form of courses, classes and modules, and their informal equivalents. These patterns and relationships are in themselves important foci for research aimed at illuminating the nature of educational experiences, thereby providing a basis for effective innovation and development.

Our notion of curriculum development, therefore, is conceived as a key activity for lecturers, librarians and administrators in their role as *educationalists*. This role is too often obscured by powerful disciplinary and professional identities, however it is an essential component of modern academic practice.

6.4 CURRICULUM DEVELOPMENT

In terms of the arguments we have advanced in previous chapters we work from a core idea of curriculum development as a pedagogical project characterised as promoting *learning for understanding (and/or perspective transformation)*.

Our approach is to present curriculum development as *a research-based investigation of the notion of curriculum within education, which explores the nature of knowledge and the value placed on learning in a given socio-cultural context*, eg, adult education (Chapter 2); higher education (Chapters 3 to 5) and their wider cultural context. We are treating development of a curriculum for information literacy as a problem to be solved rather than the adoption of an off-the-shelf solution to be inserted as and where circumstances allow. Consequently we will propose an account of curriculum which is sufficiently flexible to allow us to extend critical friendship to several major examples (Secker & Coonan, ACRL, UNESCO), whilst retaining discretion to advance new ideas of our own.

A number of defining facets of curriculum can be identified, which align with both theory and practice of curriculum creation, organisation and development in a variety of institutional settings such as schools, colleges and universities. For example, curriculum can be described in terms of combinations of the following:

- Aims and objectives expressed as both subject content to be covered and also as learning outcomes to be achieved.
- Specific subject content allied to particular teaching methods; disciplinary traditions and innovations based in research can be identified to explain decisions regarding method.
- Organisational settings and associated resource frameworks, including staffing and infrastructure (including library collections, staffing and services).
- Models derived from say transmissive and constructivist accounts of learning; Friere's (2006) critique of the 'banking' model of education is quite a useful example.
- Behaviour of teachers, learners and other participants; includes issues of optimal/non-optimal practice and experience.
- Research, development and innovation in education linked to a given curriculum project; includes disciplinary, subject-specific and other aspects of education.
- Impact of the 'digital'.

There are so many books, papers and debates about curriculum it would be unwieldy to attempt a critical review. A number of key texts can be cited for further reading however:

- Biggs (2011) is a well-established text in the UK, Australia, Hong Kong and many other parts of the world, but perhaps is not so well known in the USA. The text draws on the same tradition of social constructivism to explain and describe learning as we do in this book.
- Entwistle and Tomlinson (2007) offer a sound description of the development of ideas about the nature of learning in adults and higher education since the 1970s, with chapters contributed by many of the main contributors. For readers who are less familiar with the background to pedagogical ideas this is an essential text.

- Barnett and Coate (2005) develop the idea of curriculum as a discrete educational construct and offer a contrasting view to that of Biggs.
- Fry, Ketteridge, and Marshall (2003) adopt a practical 'how to' guide to a variety of specific teaching practices in particular disciplines; a very useful source of examples, which can be adapted to local circumstances.

All of these texts are relevant to understanding how to use the Secker and Coonan New Curriculum for Information Literacy, and similarly the ACRL Framework for Information Literacy, which we shall consider in the next chapter. However for present purposes it is sufficient to briefly summarise the main ideas put forward by Biggs.

Biggs sets out a comprehensive guide to systematic course design, engaging: aims, pedagogical design, feedback on and assessment of student learning, evaluation and improvement of practice. Biggs describes a system of good teaching and learning, which comprises the alignment of:

- Statement of learning objectives expressed through higher-order verbs such as analyse, critically evaluate, etc.
- Teaching methods designed to engage students in activities, which ensure students meet the learning objectives.
- Assessment strategies designed to both estimate student achievement of objectives, and motivate students to improve performance.

6.5 INFORMATION LITERACY AND CURRICULUM DEVELOPMENT

Our holistic perspective on curriculum and course design is highly relevant to information literacy education given the present rather fragmented situation in formal education, where the 'one-shot slot' format is prevalent, although there is growing evidence of efforts to move beyond that situation in the direction of more substantial concepts and units of curriculum. Our argument is that *if information literacy can be developed in a major operation such as an undergraduate curriculum, then it should be possible to effect a step change in the attention paid to information literacy by students, teachers, administrators, technologists, educational developers and librarians.*

In our view a curriculum for information literacy would engender the forms of intellectual development and practice, which we described in terms of critical thinking, etc. above. The enactment of such a curriculum would require teachers to renovate their pedagogical practice along the lines exemplified above (see Chapters 4 and 5 above). The outcomes would be expressed both through subject domain-specific particulars and also as a learner's ability to make critical use of knowledge and information in society, politics and so on, as discussed in Chapter 9.

The Secker and Coonan 'Curriculum for Information Literacy' makes this trend in professional thinking explicit at the present time, and is discussed below. The UNESCO 'Curriculum for Media and Information Literacy' and the ACRL revision of their standards for information literacy can also be interpreted as systematic guidance on what might constitute a 'curriculum' for information literacy in higher education and will be treated in some detail in Chapters 7 and 8. In our view the contemporary professional literature on information literacy offers significant opportunities for curriculum enquiry and development.

6.6 NEW CURRICULUM FOR INFORMATION LITERACY: A HELICOPTER VIEW FOR BUSY EDUCATIONALISTS

The New Curriculum documents offer librarians and lecturers a substantial resource for curriculum development and course design/re-design. The mix of strands, themes and specimen learning outcomes, and the examples of learning and assessment activities provide a variety of entry points to the process of course development. The presentation of the materials also suggests an acceptance of the principles of constructivism as a basis for pedagogical practice in higher education.

The New Curriculum can be accessed from two main sources:

- Online: The Arcadia Project, Cambridge University (http://arcadiaproject.lib.cam.ac.uk/historical.html), consists of an overview and implementation guidelines. This is the report of the original research project carried out by Secker and Coonan.
- Print: J. Secker and E. Coonan (2013). *Rethinking Information Literacy: A practical framework for supporting learning*. This book sets out the New Curriculum Framework and includes chapters on each of the 10 strands of the framework, written by librarians and lecturers in UK institutions who have experience of applying the framework to develop their teaching of information literacy.

The following brief summary of the framework draws on the original Arcadia research report, but is not intended to be a substitute for the rich selection of resources on offer.

6.6.1 Curriculum Aim

The principal aim is to '...help undergraduate learners to develop a high-level, reflective understanding of information contexts and issues which will empower them with a robust framework for handling new information situations, and to generate strategies for evaluating, analysing and assimilating that information as needed and at the time it is required'.

Key words allied to this aim include: 'discerning scholar', 'informed citizen' and 'autonomous lifelong learner', which give some broad indications of the kind of person envisaged as a beneficiary of more advanced information literacy.

This powerful statement of aims is firmly in the strand of information literacy scholarship, which emphasises the situated, contextual nature of information literacy as the key focus of attention. Equally it sits well with our discussion of critical thinking and metacognition in Chapters 3 to 5. As a possible guide to course design such an aim is helpful in identifying the broad directions, which a lecturer, librarian or course team should take in order to give a full account of information literacy. It is clear that such an aim could not be accommodated in a one-shot slot or even a linked sequence of slots in a course designed mainly in terms of achieving disciplinary aims.

An important consideration for practice will be the balance to be struck between this aim for information literacy and the other aims of a given course.

6.6.2 Curriculum Attributes

The curriculum has six major facets, intended to be applied flexibly:

- *Holistic*: supporting the whole process of study and research rather than just teaching traditional library skills.
- *Modular*: consisting of ongoing classes to meet the developing needs of students during their whole undergraduate career, not just one-shot sessions.
- *Embedded*: forming a salient part of academic teaching, or run closely alongside it over the course of the academic year, and with activities and problems related to students' subject context.
- *Active and assessed*: containing a significant element of active and reflective learning including peer assessment elements.
- *Flexible*: for use and adaptation in all UK higher education institutions, and designed specifically for flexible implementation.
- *Transformative*: grounded in a broad reading of 'information literacy' which sees IL not as a set of competencies but as a fundamental attribute of the discerning scholar, and as a crucial social and personal element in the digital age.

Arcadia Report P4

These facets offer a set of normative depictions of information literacy as a practical pedagogical issue in higher education. How they might be interpreted and applied in practice is a key question, but it is evident that a simplistic 'skills training' or 'one-shot slot' perspective on information literacy has been roundly rejected.

6.6.3 Using the Curriculum

There are 10 thematic strands covering a range of aspects of information literacy in educational settings:

1. Transition from school to higher education.
2. Becoming an independent learner.
3. Developing academic literacies.
4. Mapping and evaluating the information landscape.
5. Resource discovery in your discipline.
6. Managing information.
7. Ethical dimension of information.
8. Presenting and communicating knowledge.
9. Synthesising information and creating new knowledge.
10. Social dimension of information.

These themes should resonate with academics and librarians in higher education, and could be perceived in a variety of creative ways. For example, a course team interested in improving the first-year experience of students across a whole faculty might consider all or a selection of the strands for their relevance to their curriculum improvement project. By exploring the strands in relation to such an extensive educational development project, a lecturer would be sensitised to the range of options available to enhance information literacy. Equally a lecturer keen to improve the quality of final-year projects and dissertations might focus on strand 10. Such a consideration might lead to a realisation that some facets of information literacy that are needed in the final year, really need to begin being developed at earlier stages in the degree programme.

The 10 strands are grouped under five broader themes:

- Learning to learn (strands 1, 2, 10);
- Developing academic literacies (strand 3);
- Subject-specific competencies (navigating the information landscape, resource discovery) (strands 4, 5);
- Key skills, eg, searching, note taking, referencing (strand 6);
- Advanced information handling, eg, evaluation, source critique, synthesis (strands 7, 8, 9).

To illustrate – Learning to learn theme clusters strands as:

- Strand 1 – transition from school to higher education;
- Strand 2 – becoming an independent learner;
- Strand 10 – social dimension of information.

No doubt users of the Curriculum might well disagree with Secker and Coonan's arrangement of concepts, but that does not invalidate the Curriculum, and the overall emphasis within the Curriculum sits well with our own holistic perspective and our emphasis on social epistemology.

The whole framework is set out in a matrix arranged vertically by the strands and horizontally by common rows of: 'learning outcomes', 'example activities' and 'example assessment'. Within the cells one finds a number of specifics, which clarify the strand content and also provide stimulus to think in terms of how a given strand might be presented in practice. This provides users with both a 'helicopter view' of the field of information literacy and a set of particular facets, which can be related to basic pedagogical categories.

6.6.4 Implementing the Curriculum

It is very clear that Secker and Coonan are ambitious to go well beyond the one-shot-slot scenario and elevate the status of IL and those involved in teaching it. That said there is advice on planning 'sessions' in the light of the curriculum even if fuller integration is not feasible.

Advice on implementation is organised by answers to the familiar who/when/how questions faced by 'classroom teachers' in all fields of study. Also, the approach to course design assumes that it will be possible to implement the curriculum systematically throughout the years of a degree course in such a way that higher-level outcomes can be achieved iteratively over time and across different learning experiences. Some academic disciplines appear to work in this way in terms of their subject knowledge at least, for example, engineering, some sciences, and research methods teaching within social sciences. So, there may be scope to make progress more readily in such disciplines.

6.6.5 Appendices

There are four appendices dealing with:

1. Mapping the curriculum to existing IL frameworks and standards (ACRL, SCONUL, ANZIL);
2. Evidence toolkit for implementation;

3. Tips for teaching;
4. Good practice examples (discussions of case studies).

6.6.6 Commentary

Overall the New Curriculum is a substantial contribution, which pulls together earlier work on information literacy from the librarian's perspective and seeks to infuse it with ideas from educational development. Secker and Coonan clearly aim to advance the discourse and associated practice by offering a set of tools for course design, which force users to explore a greater range of options. Their approach is generative/expansionist, going beyond previous narrowly framed accounts and accepting the need for an enhanced/innovative educational basis for teaching information literacy in HE. It clearly offers a vision beyond the one-shot-slot scenario and is more obviously proposing that information literacy should be more thoroughly disseminated across courses and should be cumulative over a degree programme. This is an approach we support and which aligns with the approaches we have been discussing.

This is a practical approach, since it offers users a resource, which is grounded in established thinking, and can be approached from various entry points. It is quite possible to envisage a course team sitting down with the documents and through a process of discussion and argument, begin to draft a new design for teaching information literacy in their context. This process would be helped by reference to the examples in their subsequent book (Secker & Coonan, 2013).

Whilst we are positive about the Curriculum, we draw attention to some key shaping influences that might act to moderate or alternatively exaggerate the success of the development. First there is a substantial implied staff development challenge to be met. This applies to both librarians and discipline lecturers. For the librarians there is a need to develop their understanding of pedagogical thinking and practices, and our book hopefully goes some way to meeting that need. If librarians are to become more involved in the extended teaching roles required then they will need to develop practical experience of skills and practices going beyond the skill set of one-shot-slot teaching.

Lecturers will have to develop a commitment to implementing a curriculum for information literacy, and the New Curriculum offers a practical bridge to that commitment as it overcomes the immediate objection of a lack of guidance. However it is essential to recognise and value the fact that lecturers will have different views of information literacy than those put forward from the librarian's perspective. This is perhaps a greater potential problem than is envisaged in the New Curriculum. Our idea of *curriculum inquiry* as a form of educational practice may be helpful. If all parties to a change are willing to approach the task as a research project leading to course re-design then there is scope not simply to implement the New Curriculum set out by Secker and Coonan but to create new and more accurate designs, which cast the library and academic perspectives into a new whole.

Second, there is a level of organisational restructuring involved in any substantial curriculum innovation. There is a challenge to change attitudes and dispositions to change, which should not be underestimated, particularly when staff are under great pressure to deliver on a variety of priorities. In the event of a change being agreed there may well be resource implications to be considered. From a library perspective it may be that the greatest obstacle resides in the necessary shift in staff responsibilities and commitments from a relatively limited investment in teaching against other work, to a much greater investment of time and energy.

6.7 CONCLUSIONS

The New Curriculum is a substantial and useful contribution to the development of information literacy education. Their approach to curriculum building relates to the wider educational domain of curriculum studies, which we have outlined above and we hope that further developments in practice will exploit that relationship. We also hope that colleagues using the New Curriculum to re-design their teaching practice, benefit from the insights from psychology, which we have outlined.

We will go on to discuss the ACRL Framework in the next chapter and we suggest that readers view that North American contribution in relation to Secker and Coonan's approach from the UK tradition. It may well be that the New Curriculum is not as well known in the USA as it could be, so we hope that by treating both contributions in this book, we go some way to building valuable links.

CHAPTER 7

The ACRL (2000) Standards and the ACRL (2015) Revised Framework

7.1 INTRODUCTION

This chapter considers a significant development in information literacy (IL) coming from the academic library sector in the USA – the ACRL Framework for information literacy (http://www.ala.org/acrl/standards/ilframeworkapps#appendix2). ACRL has been a key influence on information literacy over several decades in the USA and around the world, so a shift in its approach is very significant. The impetus for change has come from ACRL's recognition of a significant shift in pedagogical practice on the part of teaching faculty in American universities. We will discuss this in more detail below; however it is worth flagging up the fact that we see much of this pedagogical shift as closely aligned to the pedagogical strategies we have advocated in earlier chapters. ACRL's adoption of the theory of threshold concepts, which originated in the work of Meyer, Land, and Baillie (2010) and others in the UK, is particularly interesting as it represents a clear move on the part of librarians to engage with ideas from educational theory as a basis for articulating their account of the learning of information literacy. It should be noted that the account of threshold concepts in the USA is based on the key contributions of Townsend, Brunetti, and Hofer (2011), Hofer, Townsend, and Brunetti (2012), and Brunetti, Townsend, and Hofer (2014). However other relevant literature includes, for example, Oakleaf (2014) and Bravender, McClure and Schaub (2015). At the time of writing in late 2015, ACRL has not retired its previous Standards and is moving forward to implement the new Framework by encouraging wide discussion amongst the libraries community and piloting of initiatives in universities. In addition, ACRL has appointed a 'case officer' with a remit to support local initiatives and organise regional and national sharing of findings.

The Framework is presented as a dramatic shift from the original Standards (2000) to reflect changes in instructional practice in higher

Copyright © 2016 A. Anderson and B. Johnston.
Published by Elsevier Ltd.
All rights reserved.
From Information Literacy to Social Epistemology
ISBN 978-0-08-100545-3

education contexts over the intervening 14 years and to signal a re-conceptualisation of IL in the light of new insights. Those insights are expressed in terms of particular pedagogical innovations, which can be observed in the practice of university and college teaching in the USA. As one might expect, a shift from a transmissive to a more 'constructivist' mode of teaching, learning and assessment is described and we will look more closely at this shift in the light of the insights discussed in Section 7.2.

The frame of reference seems to be exclusively US attendance mode institutional settings and the idea of information literacy education seems to rest on the continued efforts of librarians using an information literacy 'program' as an intervention within a pre-existing mainstream disciplinary, or cross-disciplinary, unit. Obviously this is a familiar set of circumstances and will provide a mainstream platform for development, but it may argue for investigation of the Framework in other modes such as online teaching and learning, mixed attendance modes, including short courses and courses with significant periods of placement activity.

Of equal importance is the application of "threshold concepts" to the description of information literacy and development of the Framework. ACRL identify the source of the threshold concepts idea in pedagogical research carried out in the UK by Meyer and Land (2003, 2005) as part of a project on approaches to learning in the disciplines. Threshold concepts are briefly described by ACRL as challenging 'gateway' or portal concepts, which students must navigate in order to achieve higher levels of disciplinary understanding. The criteria listed are that the TCs are: transformative; integrative; irreversible; bounded and troublesome; the bounded criterion is dropped for their purposes. We will offer our own discussion of this below.

The pedagogical attraction for ACRL seems to be that if threshold concepts for IL can be adduced and used in IL education that will be a more effective mechanism than earlier 'skills training' approaches. In addition there is a belief that promoting information literacy from a basis in threshold concepts will facilitate collaboration with disciplinary academics and thereby enhance the profile of information literacy in the academy. This seems plausible, but a great deal may depend on the authenticity of the threshold concepts for information literacy produced.

We suggest that the use of threshold concepts is a very significant development in blending ideas of information literacy grounded in the instructional practice of US academic librarians, with insights from pedagogical research. A combination of factors seems to be at work here: first, the recognition that pedagogical change is a driver for revision of the ACRL

Standards; and second the application of specific educational research to design the revision. Also, we suggest that this trans-Atlantic exchange of ideas is very significant in the development of information literacy as an international project.

At the time of writing US academic libraries and instructional librarians are engaged in a period of discussion, piloting and professional development of the new Framework. This will be an exciting and perhaps tense process. For example, it is inevitable that over the years many institutions and their librarians will have invested time, energy, credibility and resources in creating information literacy programmes and practices based in the Standards. They will be understandably wary of making significant changes to those programmes until they are satisfied that this will lead to significantly better information literacy education for their students. As a consequence it will be essential that the Framework is adopted carefully on a basis of carefully designed pilots. The opportunities for research-based educational development are very significant and if carried through should generate a substantial amount of research data about information literacy in US higher education.

In essence the Framework logic is to move from a set of prescriptive Standards primarily based in a skills-based account of information literacy, to a more holistic Framework embracing wider concepts of information literacy. In short they are moving beyond a concept of IL as a hierarchical set of skills, to a much more holistic notion of situated learners engaging with a *dynamic information ecosystem*. This suggests that IL can be implemented in curricula in more fluid forms, aligned to the notions of active, collaborative learning identified above. This move is in line with developments in the field of information literacy and we would certainly agree with that approach.

A key issue here is the extent to which professional librarians are able to carry through major educational development work, whilst managing their other responsibilities. This argues for substantial involvement of academics in the process and strong support from senior library and academic managers. The implications for enhancing the outcomes of higher education by raising the levels of information literacy in the graduate population are very considerable, so we would argue that the implementation of the ACRL Framework is perhaps going to be one of the most significant developments in the field of information literacy over the next 5 years.

We will try to add value to the project by offering a more detailed description of the question of pedagogical change based on our work in

Section 7.2 below. To achieve this contribution we have adopted the stance of 'critical friends' and approached the Framework as a 'working tool' to be critiqued and developed. Hopefully this approach will be read and appreciated as a contribution to the work of colleagues in the USA and in other parts of the world where the ACRL Standards have been influential and where the Framework is of exciting interest and debate.

The shape of our contribution:

- pedagogical changes;
- threshold concepts;
- pedagogical implications;
- definition of information literacy.

7.2 PEDAGOGICAL CHANGES

Turning to the specifically pedagogical aspects of curriculum change in higher education, in the USA since 2000, which are deemed to generate a need for a revision of the earlier Standards, a number of elements are presented as influential. It is proposed that library information literacy *programs* can take advantage of such trends to achieve greater things. It is also proposed that there is a greater need for *sense making and metacognition* to support students, which seems to relate to what we discussed in Chapter 4 using the term *epistemological development.*

We began our discussion by focussing on the list of examples of pedagogical change in the US over some 14 years since the original Standards appeared in 2000:

- Collaborative work/student teams/student collaboration in research.
- Undergraduate research.
- Integrative learning/learning communities/cross-disciplinary critical thinking.
- Focus on early years of degree programmes.
- Growth in professional masters degrees.
- IT/blended learning/MOOCs.
- 'Flipped classroom'.
- Focus on active, collaborative learning.

The list of trends seems to lack any underlying analysis or theoretical explanation to lend coherence and focus, eg, an account rooted in social constructivism to clarify where the selected 'trends' are coming from. Equally the trends/items are presented with no indication of their origins in practice, the degree of actual uptake across the sector or evidence of efficacy. These factors are evidently of significance in developing a strategy to implement the Framework. First by setting down the challenge to engage much more systematically with pedagogical research and educational development. Second by highlighting the need to carefully identify the full extent and location of the pedagogical changes driving the need to revise the standards. If it is the case that the adoption of pedagogical practices has been on a relatively small scale then it is important to estimate the scale as that will have bearing on work to incorporate the Framework.

Some questions may clarify this latter point: are particular innovations more common in some disciplines than in others? Do some lecturers embrace change more readily than others? If so, why? Are the pedagogical practices central to course design, including assessment, or are they more limited in scope? These questions speak to several major aspects of any pedagogical innovation and suggest the relevance of areas such as staff terms of employment and management structures: disciplinary differences; academic staff commitment to change; extent of the innovation in the degree programme; initial training and pedagogical development of staff; and the balance between institutional/departmental control of pedagogical practice.

These are very powerful aspects of theory, practice and traditions amongst academics in their teaching roles, and are likely to present equally serious challenges for academic librarians and their educators. In fact it may be that there is a need for a major paradigm shift in conceptualising the nature and practice of higher education for any or all of the 'trends' identified to have any significant and lasting effect.

Whilst the forgoing list of intricate areas opened up by the Framework project we should not be daunted. There is a strong emphasis on the constructs *sense making* and *critical thinking* in the proposed refocusing and that is a focus we strongly agree with.

7.3 THRESHOLD CONCEPTS CRITIQUE

The original research on threshold concepts was based on the idea that students learning disciplines at university level are faced with conceptual difficulties in the subject area, which once overcome would make a significant and permanent change in the learner's understanding of the subject. Achieving this understanding took the learner over a conceptual 'threshold' and contributed to the student becoming a member of the disciplinary community. Consequently the logic is that concentrating on these threshold concepts is viewed as a highly effective pedagogical strategy.

The thrust for ACRL is to use threshold concepts as a means to develop information literacy instruction by librarians across a variety of disciplinary curricula. This assumes that if threshold concepts can have a significant effect on disciplinary pedagogy they should also have a beneficial effect on information literacy education. So one could envisage situations where instructional librarians were designing information literacy activities based on the ACRL threshold concepts for application in disciplines where disciplinary threshold concepts had been identified and used by the lecturers in that discipline. This sounds like a complex pedagogical situation, which would need careful handling and more than simple co-ordination of effort between instructional librarian and subject lecturer. It suggests that a team approach taking commitment to a pedagogy founding on threshold concepts as the common denominator would be essential.

ACRL adopted a Delphi study to elicit practitioner input to identify candidate threshold concepts. Land et al. adduced threshold concepts by in-depth qualitative research amongst disciplinary teachers, who could identify the threshold concepts using their expert disciplinary knowledge and their insight into student learning in the discipline. This methodological difference may be significant and should be a topic of specific consideration as the ACRL discussion develops over the coming years. There may be scope for confusion in practice in situations where threshold concepts are in use for a substantive discipline at the same time they are being used to teach information literacy, for example, an economics lecturer using threshold concepts for the discipline whilst a library instructor is using the threshold concepts for information literacy. This might be addressed by co-design of courses and development of a 'community of practice' around the use of threshold concepts, which included lecturers, librarians, researchers and students. We would advocate this community of practice approach at local level and where possible suggest it be extended between institutions. There is clear scope for joint symposia and conferences around threshold concepts to share understandings, discuss practice and build a body of scholarship.

A major point to consider is that by adopting threshold concepts as pertinent to information literacy, ACRL is implying that information literacy can be usefully approached as a discipline or field of study in its own right. If threshold concepts exist within a discipline and define certain parts of the knowledge base to be learned and understood, then it follows that threshold concepts in information literacy may be viewed in the same way. This relates to the arguments for information literacy as a discipline by Johnston and Webber (2006) and Badke (2008) and is a significant avenue for theoretical development of the nature of information literacy and its place in the overall map of knowledge. In effect, information literacy becomes subject to the same kind of epistemological discourse as other disciplines.

The Framework identifies six threshold concepts and each is associated with a set of *knowledge practices* and *dispositions*. The description of each concept differs but there is a common thread, which focuses on the differences between experts and novice learners, in respect of their understandings of the concept. This might be taken as a way of expressing the notion of disciplinary learning as recruitment/induction into the disciplinary community.

The practices and dispositions differ for each concept and vary in number. They are all expressed as short phrases, which are inevitably open to interpretation, however the lists are all introduced by a common statement: 'Learners who are developing their information-literate abilities do the following:'. This is an interesting presentation and indicates commonality of learner behaviour over the six sets of knowledge practices and disposition, to the extent that specific points, and any combinations of points, all have a unified statement of objectives for action. The assumption seems to be that learning is a purposive activity, which can be described in terms of different kinds of objectives. This is in line with an approach rooted in Bloom's taxonomies of cognitive and affective objectives from the 1950s and developed over subsequent decades (Bloom, 1956, 1984).

The ACRL concepts are:

- Authority is constructed and contextual.
- Information creation as process.
- Information has value.
- Research as inquiry.
- Scholarship as conversation.
- Searching as strategic exploration.

Whilst the ACRL Framework provides elaboration of each concept it is open to readers to consider what the statements mean in their situation and the extent to which each and all of the concepts might be regarded as *threshold concepts* for learning information literacy. Given that the Framework document is to be seen as a shared document to be explored, discussed and perhaps modified in the light of collaborative discussion, it seems reasonable to attempt an initial interpretation. We have done this in the first instance by interrogating the terms of each concept statement and offer our reading as a model for others to adapt. We have restricted this first pass at the statements to interpreting one word from each concept in order to illustrate how the concepts might be interpreted; readers can compare our readings with their own.

7.3.1 Authority is Constructed and Contextual

Authority: A reasonable first response would be to think in terms of legitimacy of a text or other information entity – authorial source, reputation of publisher, currency, etc. However, it would also be plausible to interpret the word in social/cultural terms. For example, authority over the nature and presentation of knowledge in an information entity in some disciplines, might derive from a traditional white, male, middle-class power structure and this might disadvantage people who do not come from that background – authority as privilege. This interpretation would have serious implications for developing the information literacy of disadvantaged groups, or cultural groups with very different perspectives on authority.

This interpretation fits well with sociocultural accounts of learning experiences and the strategic need to promote equality and inclusion within institutions.

7.3.2 Information Creation as Process

Process: At first glance this evokes the familiar iterative process models of information literacy and therefore might be a reassuring link to well-used approaches to explaining and defining information literacy. However, it might be plausible to consider process in terms of thinking performances such as metacognition and extend the discussion from information-searching models to epistemological considerations within both information literacy and a particular disciplinary context. There would obviously be implications of interpretation of 'creation' if this line of reasoning is followed.

This interpretation is both reassuring and challenging.

7.3.3 Information Has Value

Value: Different kinds of value can be listed and discussed but it may be that the starting point is to establish the kinds of *contexts*, wherein information is valued: academic/specific task; personal life; etc. Equally there are questions of differences in value of the same information depending on the role and purposes of different persons. Epistemological questions of freedom of information versus ownership and property rights might also be raised.

This interpretation seems fairly obvious and likely to be fairly easily achieved in practice with students, for example.

7.3.4 Research as Inquiry

Inquiry: Another concept which seems to fit well to well-known models of information processes and skills of inquiry as a way of seeking out information. Equally it evokes notions of inquiry-based learning, constructivist pedagogy and therefore places educational contexts and substantial accounts of pedagogy in full view.

This interpretation is both reassuring and bridges to pedagogical thinking.

7.3.5 Scholarship as Conversation

Conversation: Whilst the scholarship word is well known and carries many presumptions about kinds of knowledge and prerequisite behaviour for scholars, the linkage to conversation might be challenging. On one reading it might be taken literally to mean a particular kind of discourse common amongst subject experts and therefore potentially exclusive unless learned over time and with substantial effort. Whilst this reading might fit well to the threshold concept notion of recruitment to a disciplinary community, it might present some challenges in showing relevance to undergraduates, particularly those taking elective courses, with no intention of taking their degree in that discipline. There would also be issues arising from disciplinary differences. For example, does a given disciplinary community regard 'conversation' as an appropriate description of scholarly communication? On this reading this is a potentially ambiguous concept.

7.3.6 Searching as Strategic Exploration

Searching: The notion of searching presents a very strong link to mainstream accounts of information literacy. This might militate against the notion of a threshold concept being in some sense troublesome knowledge, so it may be that the other two keywords are the main focus of discussion of meanings and implications for practice.

This is another potentially ambiguous concept on first reading.

7.3.7 Some Initial Conclusions

This brief analysis illustrates how rich a potential resource the Framework provides and the opportunities for greater sophistication in teaching information literacy and redesigning programmes and disciplinary courses of study. From our perspective, this is a golden opportunity for library professionals to develop an in-depth engagement with pedagogical ideas and to do this in tandem with similarly engaged disciplinary academics.

A further level of analysis of the Framework document would be to identify alignments between the key terms of each concept with the associated knowledge practices and dispositions for that concept. It might then also be interesting to see what connections might be across concepts and their knowledge practices and dispositions. It should be plain that such an analysis would be very complex, very detailed and open to differing interpretations between users. The implications for practical implementation are obviously significant and this is clearly an area for consideration as the ACRL conversation develops.

7.4 PEDAGOGICAL IMPLICATIONS

A number of specific approaches to teaching information literacy can be identified from practice and reconsidered in the light of the ACRL Framework. Such a reconsideration would go hand-in-hand with discussion of the threshold concepts and their knowledge practices and dispositions. How that might be done will be considered below in terms of educational development practices and we will give a view on the challenges for organisational development implied by the scale of change, which may be required to make full use of the new Framework.

In the first instance we will discuss three linked aspects of pedagogical activity in higher education and then look at educational and organisational development.

- One-shot slots and lesson planning: are they sufficient to the scale of change?
- Embedding information literacy in course design: constructive alignment.
- Assessment: purposes and forms.

Our basic perspective is that higher educators – lecturers and librarians alike – should take a critical approach to their teaching practice, inform practice from research on pedagogy and adopt an orientation to teaching, which includes an element of personal research and contribution to pedagogical scholarship. This is our notion of *best practice*. Whilst the *one-slot-shot* scenario is a source of frustration for library instructors who want to improve student learning in relation to information use, it remains a cornerstone of practice in many universities. Lecturers may take the view that a few sessions on particular sources and relevant searching practices are sufficient to the needs of their students and therefore be unwilling to release course time for more sophisticated interventions. In those circumstances the chances of directly assessing information literacy and incentivising students to improve their understandings and practices, are likely to be slim. Our discussion of the scope of information literacy demanded by higher education in Chapter 9 and the co-dependence of study, learning, thinking and information demonstrate our view that this is an unsatisfactory pedagogical strategy for the 21st century.

We would therefore advocate the development of new course designs, which gave prominence to information literacy as a key outcome of the course. Various options present themselves but we would emphasise prioritising a developed epistemological notion. Assessment would be a key element of our approach to course design.

The key points to bear in mind in relation to such new course design would be:

- The importance of constructive alignment of information literacy in course design.
- The importance of student time spent on tasks involving in-depth information literacy and epistemic thinking, self-regulation, etc.
- Educational development: staff development, consultancy modes.
- Organisational development: strategic policy, executive management.

Educational staff development is typically described as the provision of development opportunities for those who support learning and teaching in the university. In this case, this would be developed to support implementing information literacy within the institution. The assumption is that the status quo is not an option in the present circumstances and improving information literacy education is part of necessary change within higher education.

7.5 DEFINITION OF INFORMATION LITERACY IN THE ACRL FRAMEWORK

The draft version of the new ACRL Framework offered a new definition of IL, which would bear some serious deconstruction, as it seemed to entail a variety of aspects aimed at underpinning the shift in focus from a skills definition to what might be seen as a new orientation toward information contexts. Perhaps it is best to see the statement as a description of IL, which attempts to encompass 'contemporary' aspects of the digital 'revolution' and the accompanying information discourse into a more traditional definition of information literacy.

7.6 CONCLUSIONS

It might be instructive to speculate a little on what the scene would look like in another 14 years (2030) if the revised ACRL Framework were to be fully embraced. We contend that such speculation would immediately highlight the scale of effort likely to be involved and identify some of the practical challenges of implementation. It would also raise questions about how the kind of information literacy promised by the ACRL Framework would 'fit' into the territory of the UNESCO/IFLA/UN global perspective on information literacy as a human right, an issue to which we turn in the next chapter.

CHAPTER 8

UNESCO Contributions to Information Literacy

8.1 INTRODUCTION: EDUCATION, INFORMATION, HUMAN RIGHTS AND SOCIAL JUSTICE

In this chapter we shift focus from the psychological, pedagogical and information literacy frames discussed so far, to look at the contributions UNESCO has made to building a global platform for discussion of information literacy (IL). We will be concerned with the '...wise and ethical use...' of information in society (Johnston & Webber, 2003), viewed through the lens of one of the world's most encompassing organisations, comprising 195 member states. UNESCO is well known for prizing human rights and social justice in all its work and we applaud that commitment, although we raise various concerns regarding the constraints that hold back achievement of those commitments.

Since a major part of our contribution in this book is couched in terms of educational theory and practice, it is appropriate to begin with a brief reference to a key educational figure, Paulo Friere, whose contribution to the themes we are pursuing – education, critical thinking in and beyond formal education, epistemological sophistication and the capacity of people to take control of their lives – is substantial. His famous 1970s work 'Pedagogy of the Oppressed' stands as a key pillar of adult education and is aligned to the notions of constructivism, which we have described.

Friere's contribution to our narrative is twofold: first his ideas about learning, expressed by a critique of the 'banking' model of learning involving deposits and withdrawals, which he contrasts to a much more constructivist idea using significant person/community-centred methods; second his presentation of education as a means to improve social conditions by enabling oppressed people to recognise the nature, causes and impact of inequalities on their lives, together with the idea of improved literacy as a tool of liberation. This vision fits very well with UNESCO's humanist mission, and Friere was involved with UNESCO as, among other roles, a member of its International Jury.

Perhaps his most influential concept from our perspective is his well-known term 'conscientizacdo', taken to mean: '... learning to perceive social,

From Information Literacy to Social Epistemology
ISBN 978-0-08-100545-3
Copyright © 2016 A. Anderson and B. Johnston.
Published by Elsevier Ltd.
All rights reserved.

political and economic contradictions, and to take action against the oppressive elements of reality' (Translator's note, p. 17). The sense of empowerment through learning, knowledge, access to information and collaborative activity in pursuit of a just life seems as relevant to the global knowledge society of the 21st century as it did to the South American reality of the mid-20th century.

In this chapter we focus on a number of major UNESCO contributions to understanding information literacy in terms of a combination of humanist values applied to technological development and educational strategies relevant to 21st-century society. The key point about the UNESCO/IFLA contribution has been the elevation of information literacy from a specific aspect of local/national practice amongst librarians and educators, to a significant factor in framing international knowledge policy with implications for both the free and proprietary information sectors. This has come about through a series of linked meetings, conferences and symposia from the late 1990s through the first decade of the 21st century. We shall consider a selected group of major UNESCO contributions in this chapter rather than attempting an exhaustive account of the trajectory of UNESCO interest. Readers who would like to have a historical survey should find Horton (2011) a useful introduction.

However, it is an open question to what extent librarians, educators and policymakers have been able to implement the IL/MIL vision and the extent to which national governments/agencies have been able to adopt/adapt the key recommendations. We will consider possible explanations for this dilemma in this chapter as a preface to offering the beginnings of a solution in Chapter 9.

Key themes of this chapter include the:

- information/knowledge society discourse;
- importance of information as a socioeconomic resource;
- need for both process skills and ethical sensibility in defining and applying information literacy;
- need for information literacy to be an integral part of the curriculum for all schooling, tertiary education and lifelong learning.

This chapter deals with these themes through discussion of several major contributions to information literacy produced under the aegis of UNESCO. These include:

- Statements and Proclamations on Information Literacy arising from meetings of experts supported by UNESCO (2003, 2005);
- 'Understanding Information Literacy: A Primer', Woody Horton, prepared for UNESCO (Horton, 2007);

- 'Media and Information Literacy: Curriculum for Teachers' by Wilson et al. (2011);
- UNESCO/IFLA 'Media and Information Recommendations' (2013);
- 'Keystones to foster inclusive Knowledge Societies: Access to information and knowledge, Freedom of Expression, Privacy, and ethics on a Global Internet' (Final Study, 2015).

These contributions have been selected to illuminate our sense of information literacy going beyond the confines of the academy, the library or a given workplace, to inhabit the same territory of global socioeconomic strategy as other key areas of UNESCO's work. This is the territory we refer to as the Internet Age and extends beyond the technological infrastructures of the world wide web (WWW), and the various associated contemporary digital devices to encompass the psychological and societal dimensions of human life and communication. Combined within our concept are major social and epistemological rights including:

- Access to and understanding of the nature and value of information.
- Independence and autonomy in creating and sharing information.
- Holding and using information for lawful purposes without intrusion from the state.

These fundamental rights we associate with the notion of '...wise and ethical use of information in society', which we outlined in Chapter 1 (Johnston & Webber, 2003).

In essence we are of the view that an information or knowledge society is not simply a matter of ubiquitous information processing for educational, economic or other purposes. A modern knowledge society must also be seen in terms of human rights, their assertion and protection against oppression. To that extent we are aligned to the UNESCO position, although we are critical of the ability of states and organisations to engage such rights in the face of vested interests and outright opposition from undemocratic forces.

8.2 UNESCO CONTRIBUTION 1: PROCLAMATIONS

UNESCO has produced a number of major statements concerning IL, which are linked by a common thread of defining and advocating IL as a key facet of education and human rights in the 21st century. UNESCO's approach is liked to major visions of 21st-century reality such as: knowledge society; lifelong learning; sustainability; universal access to knowledge and information. Key statements include:

- UNESCO (2003). *The Prague Declaration* – 'Towards an information literate society'. Available at: http://portal.unesco.org/ci/en/ev.php-URL_ID=19636&URL_DO=DO_PRINTPAGE&URL_SECTION=201.html
- UNESCO (2005). *The Alexandria Proclamation on Information Literacy and Lifelong Learning*. Available at: http://www.ifla.org/III/wsis/BeaconInfSoc.html
- UNESCO (2006). *High-Level Colloquium on Information Literacy and Lifelong Learning*. Available at: http://www.ifla.org/III/wsis/High-Level-Colloquium.pdf
- UNESCO/IFLA Media and Information Recommendations (2013) – *Full text accompanies this document.*

These statements and proclamations built up a powerful rationale for the importance of information literacy in education, lifelong learning, the economy and society. They are also firmly rooted in norms of social justice and freedom of expression without fear of interference by the state or powerful vested interest groups.

Whilst couched as a high-level discourse on the nature and prospects of IL, the narrative of these statements is written to present IL and subsequently MIL as practical channels for building democratic knowledge societies, which place high value on education and social participation. These statements have been widely discussed over the years and each document provides clear guidance on the details of participants in the various contributing meetings of experts. Consequently we will not rehearse those details here, and would again direct interested readers to Horton (2011) as an entry point.

8.3 UNESCO CONTRIBUTION 2: INFORMATION LITERACY PRIMER (WOODY HORTON)

This document (2008) was prepared for UNESCO by Forest Woody Horton Jnr. The primer describes itself as: 'An easy-to-read, nontechnical overview explaining what "information literacy" means, designed for busy public policy-makers, business executives, civil society administrators and practicing professionals'. That said it is a substantial document (94 pages) of three parts:

- Background and introduction – a 21st-Century Paradigm.
- Priority Information Literacy and Lifelong Learning Initiatives in the Context of Four Key Sector Domains (the four are: Learning &

Education; Health and Human Services; Business & Economic Development; Governance & Citizenship).

- Advocacy and Awareness-Raising; Collaboration and Partnerships.

Also included are four appendices, which provide both substantial accounts of topics such as the *Information Literacy Lifecycle* and useful reference listings of terminology, key documents, models of best practice and major IL institutional resources.

As with the other UNESCO contributions the notion of knowledge societies and the power of information to enhance all aspects of life, education and citizenship are dominant. Consequently information literacy is presented as a major construct, which should be taken seriously by governments, educators and sector leaders. The overriding sense of IL is rooted in familiar notions of accessing, searching, evaluating and using information. The Alexandra Proclamation (2005) is quoted in support of this perspective on IL as a means to: 'empower people in all walks of life to seek, evaluate, use and create information effectively to achieve their personal, social, occupational and educational goals' (p. ix). Digital developments in information storage, processing and media communications are subordinated to this paradigm.

In essence a rational, positivist model of information behaviour is presented. The three major sections of the document are in line with this positivist conceptualisation and are structured to provide concretely stated recommendations for action. The *Information Literacy Lifecycle* material (Appendix B of Horton, 2008) is interesting. It consists of a matrix relating a lifecycle model comprising 11 stages (Realizing that there is a need, etc.) against five dimensions: helping human resources; tools, methods, approaches, techniques; domains and contexts, where need/problem areas arise; desired positive (functional outcomes); possible negative (dysfunctional) outcome(s). This presentation correlates certain facets of information literacy with presumed uses/settings for use. The 11 stages are virtually all expressed as 'know how/what' statements (10 of the 11 – the first in stage is expressed using 'Realize'), which suggests that IL is conceived as essentially a cognitive phenomena, thereby implying the need for learning and improving performance (as well as making mistakes obviously). Clearly it is possible to use the 11 stage statements to create behavioural objectives for study, eg, 'by the end of the session/module/course students should know …'.

This depiction resonates to an extent with the way the ACRL 2000 Standards set out a very detailed, definitive description of information literacy with sets of performance criteria, which can be deployed in terms of process models of practice, and for educational purposes mapped onto a given course design. However, it is now somewhat at odds with the new ACRL Framework (Chapter 7).

There is no explicit statement of ethical conditions, for example, or recognition of the powerful social/economic barriers to achieving information literacy under conditions of competitive economic systems and unequal societies. Equally there seems little acknowledgement of the issues of corporate control of technology and content, or state desire to restrict information access and in some circumstances to collect information about citizens without their knowledge or consent. Given Horton's expertise in information management it is unlikely that he will not have considered such matters.

In his defence he was producing material for an international organisation, with the cautions and constraints involved in that sphere of activity. Also, Horton is explicitly providing a clear guide to IL for use as: '… a ready reference for consulting from time to time by busy officials and executives having to cope every day with the complex and daunting challenges by all enterprises and institutions, public and private, *as they make the transition to Knowledge Societies at the beginning of the 21st century*.' (our italics). We might contrast this view of IL and knowledge society as largely the preserve of institutional professionals, with more radical uses of say social media by political campaigners, anticapitalism protestors and Arab Spring revolutionaries.

Horton's document is a major account of information literacy, which draws together the high-level normative statements of value with the lower levels of description of the nature of information literacy practice and how it might best be taught. Whilst Horton is working in a mainstream approach of identifying and enumerating information literacy in the form of a process model – his 11 points – he has located his work in the powerful UNESCO value scheme. One might ask why it has not had more impact?

Perhaps a clue lies in his proposal that the primer be used as a handy reference for busy officials and policymakers: Who are they? Are there specific government departments at national level charged with addressing information literacy? Are there national statements on information, which have the force of the government/state? Is it more the case that the state conceives the knowledge of society mainly in terms of digital economy/media, cultural and broadcasting organisations/regulation of Internet and telecommunications networks/educational provision and curriculum?

These questions must be answered at national level and explored in terms of the prevailing socioeconomic and political circumstances.

8.4 UNESCO CONTRIBUTION 3: MEDIA AND INFORMATION LITERACY (MIL)

Media and information literacy have developed as related but separate fields of study over many decades and media study may trace a history back to the communication studies and mass media studies of the 1960s. UNESCO has adopted the lead role for both fields over recent years and sought to combine the fields under the heading of MIL.

A recent key contribution has come from the International Federation of Library Associations (IFLA) in the form of the 'Paris Declaration on Media and Information Literacy in the Digital Era' (2014). The declaration is short and couched in affirmative language about the importance of MIL to contemporary society given the rapid advance of Internet technology. Several points from the Declaration are highly relevant to our themes:

- Importance of unifying the fields in the face of technological convergence;
- Acknowledgement that MIL must include critical thinking, creativity and ethical use of media and information;
- Recognition of the challenges raised as more and more varied sources of information become pervasive in everyday life and decision-making;
- MIL as a key aspect of citizenship in ensuring transparency by government and capacity of citizens to analyse information and deploy their analysis as part of democratic processes.

Crucially the Declaration accepts the UNESCO concept of 'knowledge societies', which we discuss in the next section, as a driving force for MIL. A final point of note is the establishment of a new organising body for MIL, the Global Alliance for Partnerships on Media and Information Literacy (GAPMIL) under UNESCO auspices. Evidently the MIL scene is developing quite quickly so it would be premature to say too much at this stage. However, it would be extremely important to ensure that future growth is first, *organic* involving a wide variety of interests, and second *balanced* to ensure that both fields have parity in any strategic discussions leading to action.

We can however say more about MIL education as depicted by UNESCO. In addition to the policy statements noted above, UNESCO has commissioned several major papers offering some detail on the concept of

MIL and a proposed curriculum for teachers, for example, Moeller (2011) and Wilson et al. (2011). These papers accept as a given that access to information, understanding of media and communication technologies, and lifelong learning systems combine as pillars of human rights in democratic societies. In this formulation, information and media awareness are essential underpinnings for citizenship. Evidently some sense of critical thinking and independent social action can be presupposed from these precepts. However, it is equally evident that an international agency will necessarily display a degree of diplomatic caution in the way it goes about describing specific examples and possibilities for such critical action.

The Moeller et al. document is very much an expression of these liberal points as social imperatives, which all parties should espouse and implement in their democratic and educational indicators of MIL. The implications of this rather bureaucratic formulation for education, pedagogy and social empowerment are clearly very substantial and by no means uncontroversial. It must be said however that the presentation of the case for MIL in the document seems to found on the notion that engaging with knowledge, media and technologies, whilst positive, is a relatively passive act of 'consumption'. This is somewhat at odds with the essential fact of the necessity of critical thinking implied by the high ideals driving the argument. Also, contestable issues of the corporate ownership, control and shaping of knowledge products are avoided in favour of a narrative of technological growth as a simple and essentially positive fact of modern life. The human dimension of the matter is presented as a set of processes and competencies, which when mastered will somehow lead automatically to productive learning and enhanced democratic participation. Much of the paper is devoted to an account of how 'indicators' of MIL might be developed and used, with limited consideration of the validity of that approach or any alternatives.

The Wilson et al. document founds on the Universal Declaration of Human Rights (article 19) and the subsequent Grunwald Declaration (1982) which... 'recognises the need for political and educational systems to promote citizens' critical understanding of the "phenomena of communication" and their participation in media ...' (p. 16). Essentially their argument seems to fall squarely in a liberal, humanist philosophy of education, which falls equally squarely in the espoused traditions of liberal, Western democracies. Given UNESCO's position in the world this is not surprising, but it is a very valuable support for the promotion of IL/MIL and a focus for any arguments as to how such laudable aims might be achieved by educational means.

The educational means proposed in the document found on pedagogical notions of:

- outcomes;
- competencies;
- a list of broadly defined main topics for teachers; thematic areas providing a framework for curriculum (Wilson et al., (2011) Table 1, p. 23);
- core teacher competencies (Wilson et al., (2011) Table 2, p. 29).

The pedagogical strategy offered includes:

- inquiry-based/student centre approaches;
- PBL;
- scientific enquiry methodology as a means of investigating media;
- case study methods;
- cooperative learning;
- textual analysis;
- translations;
- simulations;
- practical training in production of media.

None of these items is described in any detail (short paragraphs each) but it seems clear enough that they are potentially in the line of strategies inspired by social constructivism. However, as we have noted in other areas of the discussion of appropriate pedagogies for information literacy (eg, ACRL revision), there is little evidence of a developed understanding/critique of underlying psychological principles and research literature. The overall proposal of the document is that governments should adopt the curriculum into policy and implement it via a series of modules covering various aspects of teaching MIL. This is a laudable sentiment, if somewhat difficult to observe in practice.

In summation, both documents rely on relatively limited discussion of the nature of IL/MIL with rather weak definition and both over-rely on a common, and fairly simplistic notion of both constructs. Whilst this approach is admirably pragmatic in that it allows a fairly 'common sense' response, which might make sense to policymakers, it seems insufficient as an insightful vision of IL/MIL. In fairness the documents have been produced using meetings of experts, administrators, national representatives, etc. so it is probably inevitable that the outcomes will be fairly broad brush. They are also of relatively recent origin on the world stage, so it would be no surprise if they were not making an immediate impact. From our point of view this offers scope to make a useful contribution.

It is clear that there is a significant unfolding narrative of a shift in perspective to combine information literacy with media literacy within

UNESCO. Whilst relatively new, the MIL formulation seems as significant as the recent ACRL/New Curriculum contributions. It remains to be seen how the three might be brought into alignment. In the meantime we turn to the important issue of UNESCO's concept of knowledge societies.

8.5 UNESCO CONTRIBUTION 4: KNOWLEDGE SOCIETIES (2015) FINAL STUDY

This is a significant contemporary contribution drawing together the various strands of contribution over the previous decades. This work affirms the application of human rights in cyberspace and asserts that UNESCO is an appropriate platform to progress discussion of the implications of a human rights approach to the Internet. Media and information literacy are assumed to be developing and are presented as playing a critical part in the unfolding of this vision of contemporary society. Consequently the Report is a major contribution to debate on: Internet governance; promotion of freedom of expression; privacy and transparency; and protection of journalists' online sources. From our perspective this report gives further weight to UNESCO's ongoing intervention in the domain of information literacy in the Internet Age and builds on the earlier contributions discussed above. Clearly the question of the extent to which this good work can be aligned to our thinking on cognition, pedagogy and epistemology is central to this chapter and also to Chapter 9.

The Final Study was developed through the agency of a number of specialist contributions, with involvement from the Member States and including input regarding MIL. The Final Study focuses on the notion of the Internet Age and rehearses the familiar idea of a knowledge society as the characteristic of modern life. Interestingly the Report emphasises as a principle, the notion of '...a prescriptive theoretical conception of "Internet Universality", which summarises UNESCO's normative positions on the internet and highlights issues around four principles: (i) that the internet should be human rights based, (ii) open, (iii) accessible to all, and (iv) nurtured by multistakeholder participation.' (UNESCO, 2015, p. 5). These four principles have been abbreviated to the R-O-A-M principles: rights, openness, accessibility and multistakeholder participation.

The principle of universality shapes the narrative of the Report and echoes the notion of 'universal declarations' of human rights, which have helped lay down the basis of civilised life for many people around the world. However it is equally clear that such declarations are often rejected, ignored or paid token service in many parts of the world. There is clearly much to be done and it is an open question at this stage how this report can contribute to progress.

The knowledge society vision is based on four 'keystone' fields:

- Access;
- Freedom of expression;
- Privacy;
- Ethics.

These four distinct, interlinked aspects are set out as an agenda for consideration by Member States and others with an interest in a human rights' vision of the development of the Internet. That agenda could be expected to progress for building a '…free and trusted global Internet that will enable inclusive Knowledge Societies.' (UNESCO, 2015, p. 10).

The four keystones are summarised here, however we would urge readers to access the Final Study itself.

Access is regarded as universal access to all sources of information, not just the Internet, although the objective of *online access* is highly valued. Of equal importance are the implications of universal access for: freedom of information; collection and curating; respect for linguistic and cultural diversity; open source strategies; and social inclusion. Evidently there is a substantial amount of work to be done in order to meet the vision and thereby shape the Internet in the 21st century, however the four keystones do seem to offer a more focused/holistic approach to conceptualisation, which might help advocates, policymakers and practitioners navigate the complexity of the territory and the detailed material represented by the various UNESCO documents.

Freedom of expression is described holistically to encompass: right to freedom of expression online; press freedom and protection of journalists; and protection for individuals and human rights activists from repression and injustice. These topics are clearly the right kind of topics, which MIL specialists and educators need to take on board in their professional practices and to rely on when they adopt the role of activist and advocate for human rights and social justice.

Privacy is a potentially contentious area as it involves balancing the rights of individuals to keep their online activities private, alongside the rights of society and authorities to have transparency. Contemporary issues of child protection, apprehension of criminals and strategies to address terrorism are clear examples of these dilemmas.

Ethics refers to issues of design of online services and entities as well as the behaviour of individuals and groups using online communication channels. As you would expect there is a clear sense that normative shaping of the Internet should be grounded in a human rights' vision aimed at prizing the dignity of people online. Nondiscriminatory behaviour and respect for diversity are key to this ethical keystone. As with the privacy keystone, there are likely to be difficult balances to be sought and it does seem that standards of ethical behaviour and enforcement, will be quite difficult to regulate given the variation in legal systems and political authorities around the world. It may also be difficult to ensure that commercial interests operating in cyberspace will present regulatory challenges.

8.5.1 MIL in Knowledge Societies

There are several direct mentions of MIL in the text. First, in relation to privacy. The Report emphasises the need for Internet users to have confidence that their rights to privacy can be assured, otherwise there is a risk that users will be deterred from accessing information and contributing to the online world. This issue is exemplified by the serious concerns parents and teachers have in relation to children's engagement with the Internet and the risks of viewing inappropriate content or making connections with predatory or mischievous people. Any response aimed at managing the risks must inevitably involve education and awareness raising amongst children and young people. Evidently MIL education as described above would be a natural partner to such risk management. However, a study by the UNESCO initiated Global Alliance for Partnerships in Media and Information Literacy (GAPMIL) found that '...privacy is minimally addressed in Media and Information Literacy programmes, and there is a lack of understanding among educators as to what topics are privacy-related and how these apply to actual competences.' (UNESCO, 2015, p. 58). Clearly the approach to information literacy we have advocated – critical, epistemological, holistic, relational – would be a potential means of addressing the present deficiencies.

Second, in relation to the issue of developing connections and consistency across the four keystones (UNESCO, 2015, p. 76). Education in MIL is cited as an example which could be more integrated across the four keystones, with a view to generating user empowerment. This point echoes the previous concern that education for MIL is insufficiently developed and integrated into national education systems. The importance attached to this matter is evidenced by locating MIL as the first of a number of possible options for action on cross-cutting issues: 'Promote the integration of UNESCO expertise on Media and Information Literacy (MIL) into formal and informal education systems ...' (UNESCO, 2015, p. 79).

Finally, MIL is discussed in its own right in the conclusions of the Final Study. In summary, the proposal is that MIL could be a powerful vehicle to educate the public on the four keystone areas of the knowledge society. This would involve significant inclusion of MIL in school and other curricula, aligned to the workplace education and training efforts of employers. There is a serious gap in teacher education for MIL, which needs to be addressed if curriculum renovation, improved teaching practice and better uptake of new media and information technologies are to be achieved in the classroom.

It would be difficult to imagine such a project not being affirmed by all parties. However, it is equally difficult to see how the many challenges to be faced are to be overcome.

8.6 CONCLUSION

We began the chapter by referring to Paulo Friere's 1970s work on the importance of literacy in combating oppression and underpinning human social, economic and political development. Over the subsequent decades technological and other changes have redefined the notion of literacy from Friere's time. That said his vision is equally relevant to the contemporary formulation of MIL in an unequal world. To what extent has UNESCO and its contributors aligned to Friere's radical vision?

In summary, UNESCO/IFLA have pursued a rational, humanistic project to raise awareness of information literacy, combine information and media literacy and develop policy perspectives for the knowledge society of the 21st century. One might position this as a utopian project grounded in the perception of the Internet and digital technologies as key channels of human development. In essence it is a humanist technological culture based in the creation and sharing of information as major social and economic activities cast in terms of mid-20th-century social democracy. This approach is open to challenge on grounds of being a largely Western construct, which may amount to a form of imperialism or at least be seen as such in other parts of the world; Pilerot and Lindberg (2011) have argued such a case. We take their point and would add that the UNESCO project is also somewhat weak in acknowledging the prevailing inequities in societies. It is assumed that a rational, humanist perspective will be accepted by all and can be carried forward by international collaboration. However, it is clear that reality does not work that way, and that vested interests and the persistent divides between the information and educational haves and have nots will militate against any utopian vision becoming reality.

The essentially humanistic social justice values of UNESCO are challenged by the powerful influence of the vested interests of global capitalism and the organisational inertia of a corporate society (Pilerot & Lindberg, 2011). It is arguable that contemporary knowledge society is much more influenced by the marketplace and the behaviour of owners, producers and consumers of information and knowledge than the humanist vision of UNESCO. In effect, attempts by citizens to assert their human rights contradicts the neoliberal philosophy of much of the Western world. This situation can be mitigated somewhat if citizens' awareness of their rights and ability to access information about their rights – be it at work or elsewhere – can be improved. This is an obvious focus for MIL at the national level where civil society, trade unions, campaigning groups and investigative journalists, for example, can form alliances in pursuit of particular rights and justices. In addition the challenges of 21st century – regional instability; migration; global economic crisis; climate change and social dislocation – will hamper the exercise of human rights and we may need better ways of thinking and using knowledge than we have had in the past. This is a theme we will take up in Chapter 9.

A major part of the UNESCO/IFLA project is the elaboration of the educational implications of the humanistic perspective. Several headline aspects can be identified in the UNESCO contributions. First, it provides a sense of an overall curriculum consisting of the elements of information literacy written down as a coherent list. This approach is largely based on the library and information profession's concept of information literacy and places process models combining access, searching, evaluating and using information at its heart. Second, there is an emphasis on mapping this curriculum onto courses of study in the form of prescriptive documents including statements of outcomes, teaching strategies, etc. Within this approach there is a powerful emphasis on skills in searching as key foci of pedagogical effort. What is missing in both cases is any strong sense of psychological insight allied to a relatively mechanistic perspective on curriculum renovation and course re-design in practice. We see these as significant limitations.

This is a key challenge and raises the question of the extent to which the UNESCO vision can be leveraged at national/local levels and incorporated in the daily practices of librarians, educators, institutional strategists and other interested parties. We will turn to these matters in Chapter 9.

SECTION D

Social Epistemology

CHAPTER 9

Information Literacy and Social Epistemology

9.1 INTRODUCTION

In the preceding chapters we gave an account of selected concepts from psychology and applied them to information literacy in order to produce a more developed notion of information literacy as a complex, relational and holistic construct. The benefits are both theoretical, in the form of an enhanced understanding of information literacy, and the role of information in the digital age, and practical, in the form of a contribution to the practice of teaching, learning, librarianship and educational development. We also drew on our research with adult returners to higher education to explore adult learning and the experience of learning and information literacy and learning in the general population.

The key concepts from psychology that are relevant to information literacy, we argue, include: cultural tools, metacognition, critical thinking, argumentative reasoning and constructivism. Our idea of information literacy encompasses skills, processes, contexts, situated learning and notions of human rights and social justice. Our perspective is shaped by our experiences in adult learning and higher education together with consideration of wider sociocultural examples from the 'Internet Age'. We are proposing that our idea of a psychologically informed information literacy is a significantly social phenomenon and we use the construct of 'social epistemology' to express this explicitly social perspective within our thinking.

The narrative of the book is shaped to:

1. Set out the psychological material and develop a new model of information literacy;
2. Apply the psychological reasoning to pedagogy through curriculum development, course design and teaching/learning practice, to describe 'best practice';
3. Apply our pedagogical reasoning to two major contemporary contributions in information literacy – the New Curriculum for Information Literacy (which originated in the UK) and the ACRL

From Information Literacy to Social Epistemology
ISBN 978-0-08-100545-3
Copyright © 2016 A. Anderson and B. Johnston.
Published by Elsevier Ltd.
All rights reserved.

Framework for Information Literacy (which originated in the USA), which is grounded in the threshold concepts strand of educational research and development;

4. Discuss the contributions to information literacy from international organisations including UNESCO and IFLA;
5. Present our ideas on social epistemology as an advance in thinking, which blends psychology, pedagogy, information literacy and the place of 'mind' in society relevant to the Internet Age.

The present chapter presents our ideas about social epistemology and concludes by drawing some conclusions about future research, development and the implications for practice. The chapter is structured in three major sections:

- Social epistemology;
- Pedagogy for social epistemology;
- Conclusions and future agendas.

9.2 SOCIAL EPISTEMOLOGY

As we saw in Chapter 4, epistemology is that branch of philosophy, which studies the nature of knowledge and of how people come to know things about the world. In significant respects, therefore, it is the investigation of people's grasp of reality. Classical epistemology conceives of the issues involved at the level of the individual, and the relationship between the knower and what can be known. In particular, how the individual goes about acquiring knowledge and comes to arrive at a set of true beliefs (and indeed classical epistemology also wrestles with such questions as what knowledge is, what a belief is, and what truth is). Closely aligned to the issue of acquiring knowledge is the question of determining with some precision, if not finality, what out of all the knowledge available for use is of most value and utility to a person in a given context. Evidently the means (which for us include both what we have been calling 'information entities' but also other sources of information such as other people with whom we interact and collaborate) a society employs to make knowledge and information available aligned to the educational development of critical thinking are key aspects of our discussion of epistemology.

More recently, an explicitly social dimension to knowledge and belief has been acknowledged; for example, most of us rely most of the time on other people such as experts to tell us what is true, and recognition of this has led to the development of the field of social epistemology (Egan & Shera, 1952; Fallis, 2006; Shera, 1961). The contributions of Egan and Shera are particularly noteworthy given their importance in research and education for librarianship. Their work from the 1950s and 1960s is well worth revisiting in order to shed new light on the contemporary concepts of information literacy and media and information literacy, which we have been discussing. We will look more closely at their work below.

A central concern of social epistemology is the circumstances in which a person is justified in accepting the statements and opinions of others as being true (see the Stanford Encyclopaedia of Philosophy: http://plato.stanford.edu/entries/epistemology-social/). As such, this field is a very broad one, covering such matters as the aggregation of factual matters in legal contexts, the processes of knowledge acquisition and theory acceptance in science, and the acceptance as true of an item of information by an individual. Egan and Shera (1952) were the first to voice the need for 'the effective investigation of the whole complex problem of the intellectual processes of society' (p. 132), that is, the role of social factors and social institutions in people's acquisition of knowledge from other people, whether directly or indirectly via, for example, books. The Internet, of course, adds yet further complexity to the issues involved. Shera (1970) saw social epistemology as central to information science, and as having enormous practical implications for intellectual access to knowledge, and in particular he saw social epistemology as a normative enterprise that should help to specify what information services, such as libraries, ought to do in order to be more effective (Fallis, 2006).

The consensus view within classical (ie, individualistic) epistemology is that knowledge is justified true belief. This is a reasonable starting point for social epistemology to ponder; as Fallis (2006) points out, most users of libraries do not go there to seek out falsehoods or unreliable information. Instead, we can reasonably assume that they would like to acquire justified true beliefs. Social epistemologists study how knowledge creation and acquisition takes place in such social contexts. The term 'social' of course has many different senses that are relevant here, for example:

1. The transfer of information from one person to another in the sense of a book's author transferring information to the book's reader, with the aid of an intermediary information service such as a library;
2. The fact that different social groups might well have differential access to knowledge, such as disadvantaged groups having less access to information than wealthier social groups;

3. How social groups acquire knowledge, such as for example the social processes among scientists establishing a particular theory as a piece of accepted knowledge; and
4. How knowledge acquisition is affected by social and cultural factors such as income, status, and gender – for example, in the 1970s female primatologists came up with new discoveries compared to previous research undertaken by their male counterparts because they did not make the same unconscious assumptions when observing the world that their male counterparts did (Kitcher, 1994).

Floridi (2002) distinguishes between *classical* and *revolutionary* social epistemology. The classical approach follows on from classical individualistic epistemology by holding that social epistemology studies the social dimension (in all four senses outlined above) in the acquisition of justified true belief. Revolutionary social epistemology, on the other hand, views knowledge as institutionally or socially constructed.

A good example of the latter would be research on the sociology of knowledge undertaken by Latour (1987), in which, for example, it is argued that persuasion in science is not achieved solely by use of empirical evidence, but also by marshalling 'allies' of strong reputation on one's own side of a controversy. It is argued therefore that there is a social/'political' dimension to scientific practice over and above the epistemic one. A more radical view would be to claim that scientific 'facts' are not actually entities in the world but social constructions – fabrications arising from the social interactions among scientists (Latour and Woolgar, 1986; but see Stanford Encyclopaedia of Philosophy, http://plato.stanford.edu/entries/epistemology-social/ for a rebuttal). Revolutionary social epistemology therefore takes the radical position that knowledge is what is agreed to be true within a social group, rather than necessarily emphasising justification and truth as does classical social epistemology. Fallis (2006) nevertheless mounts a strong argument in favour of the classical view that knowledge is best thought of as justified true belief and that the key purpose of information services like libraries is to help the public to acquire knowledge in the classical sense, within reasonable ethical constraints such as protecting intellectual property rights.

Beyond justification and truth, there are other epistemically valuable properties of knowledge that we might value. For example, we might be motivated to seek knowledge that is highly relevant to a particular purpose that we have, or knowledge that is rich, or explanatorily powerful, or we might indeed (depending on our purposes, for example, a student writing an essay on a particular topic) be motivated to seek items of knowledge that conflict with each other. Social epistemology thus has a concern about how information services should facilitate the acquisition of epistemically valuable beliefs by ensuring that its users can access the relevant beliefs among the huge plethora of recorded material that is now at readers' disposal. This highlights such diverse issues as the design of information classification systems and the issue of how to make libraries attractive places to their users in order that users will indeed use their services.

Beyond seeking to provide users with knowledge that is epistemically valuable (in whatever sense), information services need to provide services that are fast, that serve a range of user groups and that provide reliable materials (in the sense of being likely to be true). Electronic resources clearly have many of these properties, with high speed being an obvious advantage but with reliability being not absolutely guaranteed, given the doubtful veracity of some materials that are available on the world wide web. One way of helping with the reliability issue is to provide access to a wide range of materials but to provide support to users in the critical evaluation of those materials (eg, Alexander and Tate, 1999). This links back to our discussion of critical thinking and information literacy in Chapter 3; one way of dealing with unreliability of information is to ensure that users are able to undertake a sound critical evaluation of materials encountered in their searches, and thus separate the 'wheat' from the 'chaff'. We emphasise, however, that the inculcation of such skills, properly done, requires significant input of time and pedagogical resources (see Chapter 3).

Additionally, epistemic objectives can conflict with each other. An example considered by Fallis (2006) is the 'old encyclopaedia' problem, in which there is a dilemma concerning whether a dated encyclopaedia that contains an entry with racist connotations should be retained (thereby maximising the power of the information service in terms of its making available a range of materials) or discarded (thereby increasing the reliability of the available resources by removing a resource containing information that is no longer believed to be true).

To summarise the key themes arising from social epistemology theory as described above:

- Knowledge acquisition;
- Establishing the 'truth';
- The role of 'expert' mediators;
- The experience of ordinary people;
- The relationship of knowledge to education;
- The discussion of contexts where epistemic activity occurs in society.

In the following sections we will relate the key concepts from social epistemology to the information landscape of the 21st century and the Internet Age; and consider the relationship of social epistemology to librarianship.

9.2.1 Social Epistemology in an Internet Age: Information, Communication, Economic Growth and Social Consciousness

What might be the information terrain to be surveyed by social epistemology in the 21st century? The following suggestions are aimed at grounding our ideas about information literacy in the wider population and its information ecosystem. Therefore the focus goes beyond libraries and education, although both are important parts of the social organisation of intellectual endeavour and the political direction of modern, capitalist nations.

In the first place information needs to be recognised as a central aspect of economic activity, particularly in industrial and postindustrial settings. Our view is that economic shifts from an agricultural to an industrial and thence to a knowledge economy, have been facilitated at every stage by concomitant changes in the nature of information activity and technologies for handling information. Thus whilst the agricultural economy was mainly supported by verbal and written means of communication about production cycles, markets, prices, technological developments and the like, industrialisation was enabled by the electric telegraph and a variety of specialist information products aligned to financial markets as well as directly to productive activity. This is particularly evident in the obvious need for such developments in the information sphere to permit international trade, the organisation of world markets, the functioning of stock exchanges, banks and other financial supports to enterprise.

For example, it became essential that the flow of specialist kinds of information such as raw material prices, stock market quotes, credit ratings, exchange rates and details of technological innovation, could be organised and integrated to flow rapidly and efficiently. Some of this information was in hourly and daily circulation via telegraph and later telephone and telex systems, but also appeared in print form in specialised financial newspapers, commercial journals and the internal communications of competing enterprises. Such content could also be aggregated to form historical datasets for predictive purposes and also as aids to retrospective academic analysis. Other specialised forms, such as patents, technical reports, blueprints and so forth circulated more slowly and access was often conditioned by legal constraints designed to protect the property rights of the owners of the information and their ability to exploit the information for competitive advantage. Over the 20th century these activities developed exponentially and became an economic sector in their own right embracing newspapers, broadcasting and latterly the Internet and digital communications. Clearly the proliferation of scientific and technological information in universities and research institutes added considerably to the scale of the information enterprise, a process accelerated by the needs of the two World Wars and the subsequent long period of Cold War.

This economic information phenomenon was mirrored in society, to some extent, by the growth of information in relation to education, political emancipation, freedom of speech and access to the widest range of cultural experience. It seems evident, however, that the social and economic inequalities of uneven economic growth, within nations and between nations, were replicated in differential access to information and education by their citizens. This is not to say that people were entirely subjugated by economic forces, although at various points the levels of exploitation and outright oppression amounted to subjugation. As people were brought into new forms of economic and social relationships they began to develop better understandings of their circumstances and to develop new ideas about themselves and their possibilities. Where education and access to information were possible, the human capacity to learn, to organise and to rise above earlier forms of social life was enabled.

As with all technological 'revolutions' the advent of the Internet and the various digital devices and systems of the late 20th and early 21st centuries have been described in both positive and negative terms (see, eg, Papacharissi, 2002, for a balanced review of both perspectives). Typical strategies have been to align the technologies with gains in cultural experience, democracy, freedom of speech, social connectivity and economic growth. The UNESCO contribution on the knowledge society discussed in Chapter 8 can be seen in this light. By the same token critics point to the downsides of economic exploitation of producers, excess profits by major companies and individuals, intrusion on personal privacy by governments and a variety of social pathologies associated with abuse and exploitation of the technologies: Keen (2015), Lanier (2013), and Morozov (2015).

An interesting contemporary contribution to the debate is that by Mason (2015), who argues that the digital revolution can be conceptualised in terms of socialism and socialist politics. Mason reprises the various socialist thinkers from the 19th century onwards, and envisions an alternative future for the 21st century wherein the Internet creates the possibility of a different social consciousness rejecting contemporary neoliberal orthodoxy in favour of a more communitarian future. Mason's detailed argument is too complex to reproduce here, but his blending of socialist economics and philosophy to present a new vision of the Internet Age is worth reading as an antidote to simplistic accounts of our times in what is now undeniably a digital age.

No doubt the debates will continue and should rightly form part of the discussion of the nature and practice of information literacy. We propose that the values and appreciation of information and knowledge held by citizens in the 'Internet Age' reflect the social epistemology of our times. For example, take access to information about 'news' in the modern world. The digital technologies support an array of possible engagements with news stories, opinions, factual data, leisure content and, crucially, advertising. In the past a print newspaper or magazine would source news, write copy, print text, advertise goods and offer opinions all within paper's covers. This remains a feature of the epistemological landscape, but it is complemented by a very fluid exchange of content between websites, blogs, twitter feeds, video sites, broadcast media and so on. Evidently the boundaries between 'news' content, social life, political persuasion and engagement in society have become somewhat blurred by the speed and ease of information exchange in the Internet Age.

9.2.1.1 The Internet Age

Terms such as the 'Internet Age', the 'information society' and the 'knowledge economy' have entered the language over the last few decades, and have a variety of connotations, depending on one's social, economic and educational position. For our purposes, we will use the 'Internet Age' to signify the growth of the Internet as a key feature of global information activity in all spheres of life, linked to a fast-moving market in digital devices, which afford users access to information for a variety of economic, social and educational purposes. In effect the Internet Age is viewed as a new stratum of *reality* comprised of information, which is rapidly redefining our notions of knowledge and the place of knowledge in society. We identify four key features of the Internet Age.

First, there is a global technological industry, with companies such as Google, Facebook, Amazon, Apple and Microsoft, exploiting the possibilities of digital technology to create jobs, goods, services and wealth. This industry has proved capable of significant business growth and social impact, despite successive economic crises, including the 2001/2 dotcom crash and the 2008 global financial crisis. Whilst there is a degree of churn in the technological market place, it seems evident that the Internet-based industries of the early 21st century can be likened in historical importance to the older steam-, oil- and electricity-based industries of the 19th and 20th centuries, many of which are now in severe decline.

Second, the technological businesses have generated a huge user population of suppliers, consumers and advertisers. The resulting market is differentiated to include sectors specialising in: news; entertainment; consumer goods; and education. Equally important is the reliance of financial services on the Internet and digital technologies for fast and reliable transfer of information about markets and also for procedures to manage business transactions. All kinds of organisations from supermarkets to steelworks are reliant on digital technologies to control production, secure their data and conduct their information management; and staff members at all levels can hardly imagine their daily working lives without digital technologies. Over the next few years it is likely that more and more homes will become suffused with digital technological devices, with computers and phones sitting comfortably alongside heating/lighting systems, kitchen appliances, security sensors, etc. In effect, the near-future technological ecosystem will be defined by the increasing numbers of devices, which are connected to the Internet to form a global environment connected by data and information sharing.

Third, there are potential downsides, most obviously the creation of huge monopolies in information, which might tend to undermine any notion of free social control and direction of the Internet's power. Such monopoly positions might be seen as a threat to realising the humanist vision of UNESCO. For example, Google currently has the monopoly position in searching and is also a massive advertising business, which is key to the interface between potential consumers and suppliers of everything from travel services to information about university courses. This situation is a far cry from the concept of freedom held by the Internet's founder, Tim Berners Lee. Of course a serious aspect of this reality is the potential for inequality across social groups in both access to and educated/literate use of the Internet. Inequality has a variety of faces: exclusion from the workforce and marketplace due to lack of knowledge and skills; marginalisation in communities due to digital exclusion; and underdevelopment of human potential.

It can be argued that a combination of market forces and education will iron-out any such inequalities and that may be so. Allied to concerns over the corporate monopoly of the Internet there are concerns being raised about state monopoly of information about the activities of citizens and social groups. One key concern is the perception of a growing surveillance state, gathering information about individuals and organisations via digital technologies, for example, the controversy over Wikileaks. Whilst many nations have clear laws on privacy and freedom of information, there is a perception that the balance of power lies with state organisations over the citizen (Keen, 2015; Lanier, 2013; Mason, 2015; Morozov, 2015).

Fourth, despite the emphasis on corporate and state activity as a major shaping force in the Internet Age, it is worth noting that one of the world's largest information resources (Wikipedia) was created, and is produced and maintained freely, by volunteers. This seems to be much more in line with Tim Berners Lee's vision of information flowing freely around the Internet affording knowledge and community to all. Wikipedia also radically reinvents the notion of the encyclopedia stored on a library shelf, to one of global availability of information structured by the encyclopedia form, but released from the constraints of the printed page and updated by the day rather than the decade. Close observation of some sites can be akin to following the flow of argument, correction of errors and presentation of evidence, which characterise well-run student tutorials and academic seminars. People are not so much consulting a reference work as engaging in active and collaborative learning. This seems entirely in line with the account of constructivist pedagogy, which we have been developing throughout this book. In effect Wikipedia is a plausible candidate to represent the notion of social epistemology in action in the Internet Age.

Taken together these four aspects may suggest that whilst the Internet Age looks like earlier stages of social and economic reality in the adoption of monopoly and market capitalism, with its attendant contradictions and tensions, there is an equally powerful strand that is communitarian and collaborative. Wikipedia is a large-scale example of this development, however the potential for further developments in that direction are present. The everyday networks of computers, phones and tablets connected to the Internet are embedded in human agency, motive and potential to create new forms of collaborative working and association. A relevant example would be the formation of spin-out enterprises, both private and social, from existing companies, to create new business based in more collaborative production and sharing of risk and reward. This also includes lower-level and shorter-term computer-based collaborative tools such as computer-supported communication systems, computer-supported collaborative work, computer aids to collaborative writing and so on.

This account of the Internet Age and its potential to underpin new forms of social and economic reality raises significant questions for education and information literacy. Principally – *how does education prepare people for a potential new form of economy and what part might information literacy play?* We will explore this question in the following sections.

9.2.2 Social Epistemology and Librarianship

Shera's work (1965) demonstrates the importance of librarians to the organisation and use of society's knowledge resources. Shera's account of human information behaviour, both for personal satisfaction and societal advance, led him to call for:

'… a new discipline, perhaps a science of communication. This is not to be understood as a plea for a reworking of the old field of mass communication, or even for more communication studies, so-called, with which the language arts have recently been identified. We are here concerned with an epistemological discipline, a body of knowledge about knowing itself. The manner in which knowledge has developed and has been augmented has long been a subject of study, but the ways in which knowledge is coordinated, integrated, and put to work is, as yet, an almost unrecognised field for investigation.' …'The new discipline that we here envisage (and which, for want of a better name, we have called *social epistemology*) should provide an effective framework for the effective investigation of the entire complex problem of the intellectual processes of society – a study by which society as a whole seeks a perceptive relation to its total environment.' (pp. 15/16).

One thing is clear from Shera's work in the 1960s, and it is that librarianship emerges as a predominantly social activity and a key aspect of his idea of social epistemology. That social activity can be observed in terms of the role and practice of librarians and libraries in providing access to books, knowledge, information, and also in giving users advice on how to gain access to these resources. The social location of library contributions to the organisation of knowledge for access and use can also be considered in terms of the traditional expectation of citizens that libraries are a 'free' public good with the necessary status, funding and accountability to fulfil those expectations. As to the provision, development and regulation of libraries, this may be seen as being best managed in the public interest through the state, national and local authorities in respect of a nation's school, public, academic and national libraries.

This account creates a varied practice, so information literacy would be seen as a greater or lesser priority, depending on the sector and specific contexts. As such librarianship deserves a voice in the debate on the nature of the 21st century's information culture. This view is underpinned by subsequent developments such as: the UNESCO/IFLA statements on the nature of the situation of media and information literacy; statements, professional development and advocacy by national professional associations; national and international conferences on information literacy and many other aspects. Whatever else librarians do in the 21st century, we suggest they must be able to show professional commitment to a developed concept of social epistemology grounded in Shera and Egan's groundbreaking work but updated to embrace the sociotechnical advances since the 1960s and 1970s along with the economic and political changes of the period.

Professional commitment on the part of librarians can be viewed in relation to how the popular perception that digital sources are becoming the new normal, and the impact of austerity in the UK, and elsewhere, influences how funding for library services is decided. Austerity politics is aligned to a market-driven notion of services being primarily delivered to consumers via private enterprise, or voluntarily via 'big society'-type initiatives; this latter has been particularly evident in the field of public library service in England. Consequently the operationalisation of professional commitment will not be easy in a period where digital technologies and the Internet are widely claimed to be sufficient to most information needs, and libraries are under severe funding constraints.

Whatever the professional content of education for librarianship over time, our suggestion is that its pedagogy should align with the ideas of constructivism outlined in Chapter 5. Thus librarianship students should be experiencing the kind of approaches to teaching and learning discussed in those chapters. Equally postgraduate research needs to offer opportunities to explore information literacy in the widest variety of contexts and should not be restricted to specifically library settings. Both of these suggestions indicate the need for iSchools and librarianship departments in higher education to be staffed by innovative lecturers with a strong commitment to research and postgraduate supervision.

The organisation of libraries will need to be revisited in order to rebalance the mix and importance of current activities if information literacy is to become a predominant feature. In practice each library has to deal with providing access by managing: space; opening hours; acquisition of resources; classification, cataloguing and display of those resources; provision of advice, reference and user education (or information literacy in current parlance) and many other familiar features of libraries. They must also keep up with developments in the information and publishing industries, aligned to demands for new digital services from their users. Meeting these requirements is expressed in strategic plans, budgets, spaces, staffing complements, organisation charts, technological infrastructure, physical management and accountability to the parent organisation – university, local authority, school, etc.

These arrangements may not necessarily prize an information literacy programme as a major operational mission of a given library, although there will likely be something recognisable as such in institutional policy statements and so forth. For example, a library policy or a university statement of graduate attributes may refer to 'information literacy'. Clearly there is much scope for mismatch between what specific libraries can realistically achieve and what national bodies such as ACRL, and organisations such as UNESCO advocate. Consequently it would be no surprise if important advances such as Secker and Coonan's New Curriculum and the ACRL Framework discussed in Chapters 6 and 7 were adopted slowly in practice, despite their evident utility.

In terms of libraries in educational settings it is possible that under the pressure of rapidly developing electronic access to digital resources the library will come to be seen as of decreasing importance in meeting information needs. These are tensions to be managed, but one aspect, which is particularly relevant to our perspective, is the role of librarians as educators. There is nothing particularly new in suggesting that librarians in educational institutions should be 'teachers', however their role has tended to be restricted to the forms of teaching necessitated by the limited time allowed them by the disciplinary teachers and lecturers. The 'one-shot slot' in other words. Clearly, this position is being challenged by librarians. However, it seems clear that a major effort of strategic organisational development involving several different groups of staff will be required (see Chapter 4).

Such an effort of organisational development will need to have the support of organisational leaders from outside the library. Different organisations will approach the task in line with their priorities but a key is the concepts of information, knowledge and information literacy held by leaders. This suggests the need to create forms of staff development which address conceptual change in relation to information literacy as well as any particular programmes of skill development. In effect this would be a move towards developing information-literate institutions. In terms of organisational development, let us turn from higher education to the field of public library service and how it might develop in the Internet Age.

9.2.2.1 Smart Libraries for Smart Cities: A Possible Future Direction for Information Literacy in Urban Spaces

The source of this example is a paper to the ECIL conference by Jerkov, Sofronijeic, and Straniic (2015) on the theme of the library as an 'information literacy hub' for a new kind of city. The notion of Smart Cities has arisen in debate on the nature of technology and its application to urban settings such as cities, for example: Albino et al. (2015), Komninos, (2014), and Min (2012). In essence the debate revolves around the integration and co-dependencies between: digital technology, urban design, transport and other services, local economic activity and the implications for human living in cities. The relationship to information literacy is focused (in the paper) on the need to revise the position and activity of public library services in Smart Cities. The basic argument is that as the complexities of technological, economic and social integration grow, this changes the profile of information literacy amongst citizens.

A particular need is for people to update their knowledge of technology and their capacity for inclusion and engagement in the digital realities of urban living. Information literacy in such circumstances becomes a very complex pattern of digital interactions with services and systems aligned, or misaligned, to a person's knowledge of the nature of information, their sensitivity to information contexts and their ability to manage and express themselves along digital channels. In practice information literacy would be an integral part of both everyday life in an urban setting and also of the more specialised contexts of work, education, health care, etc.

It seems plausible that public libraries should be an integral part of the development of information literacy amongst the inhabitants of a 'Smart City' by offering a range of services to update and evolve people's information literacy. The library could become a site where new technologies could be accessed and patrons could engage with training and development activities. A key element of such developments would be a commitment to participation and collaborative development of the system by citizens.

Many public libraries already offer access to computers, the Internet and other digital affordances together with some degree of training. However, the impact of such provision may be relatively small at present. There is also a growing concern in the UK that as the new system of universal (welfare/social security) benefits requires claimants to interact with the system online in order to make claims and also to engage with Job Centres to comply with mandatory job application targets, which requires searching job databases, creating CVs, applications and so on, again online, there will be increased demand on relatively underprepared public library services as more people from disadvantaged groups are forced to 'go online' in order to secure benefit income and apply for jobs. Many libraries have time limits on computer access, which represent a constraint on the realisation of the 'Smart City' idea. If in addition substantial numbers of members of the public are seeking more help and advice from librarians in filling out forms and so forth, the resourcing constraints become even more acute.

Whilst the collective, public sector ethos of the Smart Cities idea seems to be in line with the collective, volunteerism displayed by Wikipedia as discussed above, the Smart Cities/Libraries idea raises a set of critical social issues. First, the creation of Smart Cities is essentially a matter of market economics, with large companies controlling the design and development of infrastructure and information services. The interactions between energy provision, transport and data services are at base commercial interactions between profit-making, often international, businesses and local city administrations. Whilst this may be the best way we have at present to innovate urban infrastructures it is a very different model to a knowledge space like Wikipedia. Whilst small-scale, information business start-ups might offer some mitigation of 'big' corporation influence, it is equally possible that they would be elbowed out of the market or simply acquired by bigger organisations unless they rapidly develop into large corporations themselves.

The governance of Smart Cities is likely to be a combination of municipal democracy, conditioned by the influence of the private companies providing traffic management systems, data control and management, etc. Questions arise regarding whether such technically, legally and financially complex situations could be managed by 'bottom-up' participative arrangements.

These are major issues in the definition of information literacy in the 21st century and we suggest that our concept of social epistemology is a useful tool in pursuing an answer to the questions raised by the notion of a Smart City. We will say more of this in our discussion of pedagogy for social epistemology.

9.3 PEDAGOGY FOR SOCIAL EPISTEMOLOGY

Learning in the Internet Age: applied social epistemology?

How does the Internet Age change the process of learning compared to what it had been in the pre-Internet Age? Learning is obviously an ongoing process of intellectual and practical development aligned to the needs of individuals and their societies. However, education also has a larger connection to both understanding and changing society, in effect playing a direct role in channeling and comprehending transformational change. As society changes the ways in which work is carried out, value created using business models employing digital technology, for example, the notion of relevant education needs discussion. In essence education is not simply being 'about' gaining relevant skills but crucially engaging critical analysis of the full range of social implications of the technological transformations. These relationships pose questions about social epistemology concerning: formal schooling, tertiary education, workplace learning, online systems and informal and community services.

Equally the new technological affordances are available to learners and educators to create fluid information environments within formal education and less formal lifelong learning. A particular site of this enquiry is what MacLellan and Soden (2008) described as: '..pedagogies that help learners to reassert the political dimensions of self-direction by bringing into their *critical consciousness* those assumptions, beliefs and values which have been uncritically assimilated and internalized' (our italics).

Our argument in outline is that whilst the Internet Age is associated with a polarised discourse of positive and negative accounts conducted between highly educated and committed partisans, there is scope and a need for a psychologically informed contribution, taking information literacy as a key factor. We suggest that in the internet age it is the development of the individual and community capacity *to organise and use knowledge in society*, that is the key objective of education. The echo of Shera's words above should be clear. In the past when educators and librarians filled key roles, and to an extent still do, there is now a potentially huge population that can become more epistemologically sophisticated, given access to powerful cultural tools in the form of the Internet and digital technologies.

In order to outline how such a pedagogical change might be effected in practice we present scenarios for university education and lifelong learning respectively. First, we reprise our presentation of constructivism as the pedagogical heart of organisational and societal development.

9.3.1 Constructivism

In earlier chapters we have outlined a broad shift in pedagogical thinking and practice from transmission of information by teachers to learners, towards a pedagogy based on the ideas of social constructivism. Constructivism is typically represented as a theory of learning in which learners construct their understandings via critical engagement with knowledge to build personal structures of knowledge. Rather than simply receiving information the learner seeks meaning from a variety of information sources and discussion with others. Teaching practice shifts from lectures and other transmittal modes, to problem-based, collaborative and experiential designs for learning. Tanner (2012) presented a concrete example of constructivist ideas in practice, which we discussed in Chapter 4.

This shift in thinking is an important development for information literacy education for two reasons. First, constructivism offers insights into how information literacy might best be taught by lecturers and librarians. This implies a need to devise educational and professional development training for librarians, to provide opportunities to develop a capacity for constructivist practice. Second, as constructivist teaching strategies take hold and become mainstream in higher education, the change pressurises information literacy specialists to revise their perspectives on the nature of information literacy teaching.

This shift in perspective is exemplified by the development by ACRL of the new Framework for information literacy, which we discussed in Chapter 7. In effect, ACRL was responding to changes in the pedagogical thinking, practice and culture of American higher education when it decided to revise the earlier Standards. In both cases it is important for librarians with teaching responsibilities to explore constructivist perspectives, investigate how they might be applied to their own work, and engage in pedagogical debate with subject lecturers, many of whom will be experiencing a similar pressure to revise their practice. This process is already evident in the literature, for example: Bruce (2008) Elmborg (2006), Harris (2008), Hepworth and Walton (2009), Jackson (2007), Johnston and Webber (2003), Limberg, Alexandresson, Lantz-Andersson and Folkesson (2008), Lindstrom and Shonrik (2006), Medaille and Shannon (2012), Mounce (2010), Pritchard (2010), Rosling and Littlemore (2011), Walton and Hepworth (2011), Webber, Boon and Johnston (2005), and Webber and Johnston (2000).

As constructivism comes to hold a preeminent position in guiding curriculum renovation, and associated organisational development of teaching practice, course design and technological innovation, it makes considerable sense to engage with those ideas in depth. This course of action can take many forms, but we suggest that approaches which encourage significant engagement with the ideas of constructivism described in this book are required. For example, development projects aimed at changing the design of whole courses; research into constructivist pedagogy in different disciplinary contexts; and of course doctoral studies of constructivist approaches to information literacy.

Underpinning constructivist approaches to teaching and learning is the development of metacognition, represented as the learner gradually gaining greater awareness of his/her ways of thinking, leading to greater capacity to regulate those processes. Metacognition is now a prominent force in the debate on how to improve student learning and should be explicit in course designs, and teaching, learning and assessment practice. Developing metacognition amongst learners can be operationalised by a variety of mechanisms; reflection, discussion and analysis of the cognitive structure of a given experience are general tactics. Again Tanner (2012) provides a good indicative guide based on practical teaching experience. Equally important is the exploration and enhancement of teaching practices appropriate to a constructivist thinking. Simply advocating a move from 'transmission' to 'facilitation' is insufficient and it is essential for teachers to develop the personal characteristics to provide effective teaching practice.

9.3.2 Information Literacy Teaching Within Universities

We gave some examples of specific whole-course designs using constructivist strategies in earlier chapters. However, scaling up from single modules or classes, involves an additional set of organisational requirements, opportunities, constraints and challenges. In order to highlight a possible way of meeting the challenge of scaling up in general, we summarise a substantial project from the experience of one of the authors (Johnston & Watson, 2009). This project was developed in the University of Strathclyde Business School (SBS) and was spread over a decade from the late 1990s.

The focus of the project was to greatly extend student development of management capacity, using a largely experiential and problem-based design based on the principles of constructivism. The programme was known as the Management Development Programme (MDP) and took the form of a sequence of three credit-bearing modules sequenced over each of the first, second and third years of the honours programme (Johnston & Watson, 2004, 2006). It was designed as a compulsory part of the degree and involved all SBS undergraduates, typically around 500 students in each year cohort.

The pedagogic strategy driving this project mirrors many of the points we have been making in earlier chapters: going beyond basic 'skills' accounts of complex phenomena; innovating the course design using collaborative learning, projects and varied student interactions with information; and treating the curriculum project as a research activity aimed at illuminating pedagogical practice as well as delivering teaching. Over the years we derived four key principles of educational and organisational development, which we suggest can be applied to an information literacy initiative and they are presented here in order to suggest a way of conceptualising a major scaling up of an information literacy initiative to a whole faulty/school level. The four principles are:

- Organisational commitment;
- Teaching team with shared pedagogy;
- Active learning design;
- Employer partnerships.

In the first instance a significant *organisational commitment* is required, going beyond general inclusion of information literacy in mission statements linked to a number of small-scale, uncoordinated initiatives. Key features of such a commitment would include: first, an environmental scan to establish the nature and benefits of information literacy in the Internet Age; the account of the Internet Age above and the UNESCO works discussed in Chapter 8 represent the kind of features which might be captured by such a scan. Second, a concrete strategic direction from the senior management to institute a major initiative, together with the staff and other resources required. Third, a major course design/redesign project involving academics, librarians, educational developers and technologists is required to create a relevant curriculum. Finally, the course should be compulsory for all students to maximise the benefits and substantially increase the number of graduates with significant understanding and expertise in information literacy.

In order to operationalise a course on this scale a *teaching team with a shared pedagogy* is essential. Obviously we would advocate the adoption of a pedagogy grounded in constructivist theory and strategies. However, we would not underestimate the practical challenge of creating and sustaining a team over a period of years. Clear management and staff co-ordination are essential, as is a serious commitment to staff development through focused effort and regular, in-depth review of practice. The nature of an *active learning design* should be reasonably clear given the discussion of constructivist strategies in earlier chapters. However, one would expect to see not only student teamwork and so forth, but also an explicit focus on developing metacognition. The employer partnerships principle is hopefully self-explanatory and each institution will identify graduate employers they wish to engage with. We suggest that the more involved employers can become in shaping the course and getting involved with students the better. For example, by providing authentic problems for project working, giving advice and feedback to students and commenting on student presentations.

What we have described as a scenario for major innovation in a university is evidently a great step forward from 'one-shot' teaching slots, or even the introduction of dedicated elective modules. It should be clear that undertaking this scale of change cannot be achieved through the efforts of a small group of committed librarians and lecturers. If an institution sees major changes in its environment – Internet and technological advances, labour market demands on graduates and perhaps competitor behaviour – then its leaders have an obligation to make the necessary commitment. Senior management commitment is essential to the shift in pedagogy and staff commitment to that change should be incentivised and rewarded. It is at this scale of institutional change that contributions like this, the New Curriculum for Information Literacy, the ACRL Framework and the various UNESCO initiatives might make the largest impacts by providing the arguments and conceptual tools to enable change in practice.

9.3.3 Information Literacy Teaching Within Lifelong Learning Contexts

Lifelong learning offers a more diffuse and complex situation for developing information literacy than is offered by redesigning the structures and pedagogy of university undergraduate education. Since lifelong learning doesn't have institutions of the scale and resourcing of universities, schools, colleges or workplace training it must remain speculative as to how to proceed. If the approaches advocated by UNESCO for developing education for MIL could be cascaded and developed at national level and through the general population, then progress would be made. The case study presented in Chapter 2 suggests a more fluid relationship between higher education and the population, which constitutes the potential catchment of lifelong learning. Whilst information literacy and epistemological development was muted in the particular case it was shown that there was potential for improvement. Perhaps if we were to develop a curriculum for MIL through the forms of new courses offered by centres for Lifelong Learning in higher education some progress might be made. This approach would require national leadership of MIL education aimed at involving substantially greater participation than is currently observed.

An obvious strategy would be to use the Internet and digital technologies as channels for MIL education. MOOCs are a contemporary focus for such a strategy, however there is still the question of leadership, development of the curriculum and creation of the MOOC. Given the availability of platforms such as Future Learn (see https://www.futurelearn.com/) and Coursera (see https://www.coursera.org/) with growing expertise in both design and use of MOOCs for a variety of subjects and topics. Several examples relevant to MIL have begun to appear, see:

http://elab.lms.athabascau.ca/
https://ecolearning.eu/
http://metaliteracy.cdlprojects.com/
https://www.futurelearn.com/courses/academic-integrity
http://www.unesco.org/new/en/communication-and-information/capacity-building-tools/media-and-information-literacy/.

The UNESCO sponsored GAPMIL, which is described in Chapter 8, also has a relevant site:

http://www.unesco.org/new/en/communication-and-information/media-development/media-literacy/global-alliance-for-partnerships-on-media-and-information-literacy/.

In any case, at the level of the national state it would be necessary to consider whether it would be possible to restructure the social investment in education to create a new infrastructure for 'whole *community* learning'. In essence it would be a case of producing new additional funding or repurposing some of the current social spend on education to create a 'citizens' curriculum' for the Internet Age. This idea might be dismissed at first glance as unrealistic in times of austerity; however, if we are serious about uprating the level of critical thinking and information literacy in the general population as a necessary characteristic of modern democracy, then it is worth thinking through. In Chapter 8 we considered UNESCO's powerful ideas of human rights and social justice in relation to MIL and concluded that the contribution would offer a sound basis to begin a national debate.

To outline some possible directions for debate, first, it would be essential to make out a case for developing the MIL curriculum as a social benefit, which could be debated and, if accepted, developed. Second, there would need to be a focus for practical development and in the first instance that would require the creation of an organisation. It is not clear as yet whether that would be done by extending the remit and resources of existing organisations or by the creation of a new organisation or network of organisations. Finally, one could envisage making a start by creating a number of focused pilot projects to examine options and gain useful experience.

9.4 CONCLUSIONS

In this book we have explored a number of themes relevant to information literacy education, and it is our contention that there is scope for a wider debate regarding how to bring the various contributions of UNESCO, ACRL and Secker and Coonan together. An essential component of that debate on media and information literacy education needs to focus on the potential relevance and utility of the areas of psychology we have reviewed: critical thinking, epistemological thinking and metacognition. We offer this proposal in the spirit of critical friendship, and look forward to colleagues joining the debate with us.

REFERENCES

Abrami, P. C., Bernard, R. M., Borokhovski, E., Wade, A., Surkes, M. A., Tamim, R., et al. (2008). Instructional interventions affecting critical thinking skills and dispositions: a stage 1 meta-analysis. *Review of Educational Research, 78*, 1102–1134.

Albino, V., Berdardi, U., & Dangelco, R. M. (2015). Smart cities: definitions, dimensions, performance and initiatives. *Journal of Urban Technology, 21*.

Alexander, J. E., & Tate, M. A. (1999). *Web wisdom*. Mahwah, NJ: Erlbaum.

Anderson, A., Cheyne, W., Foot, H., Howe, C., Low, J., & Tolmie, A. (2001). Computer support for peer-based methodology tutorials. *Journal of Computer-Assisted Learning, 16*, 41–53.

Anderson, A., Howe, C., Soden, R., Halliday, J., & Low, J. (2001). Peer interaction and the learning of critical thinking skills in further education students. *Instructional Science, 29*, 1–32.

Anderson, A., Johnston, B., & MacDonald, A. (2012). Patterns of learning in a sample of adult returners to higher education. *Journal of Further and Higher Education*. Published online 23/10/2012 at http://dx.doi.org/10.1080/0309877X.2012.726971.

Anderson, A., Johnston, W., & McDonald, A. (2011). Access in a new age of Austerity: experiences of students participating in the Pre-Entry Access course at the University of Strathclyde. In *Paper presented at the Annual Conference of the Universities Association for Lifelong learning, Stirling, Scotland, 22nd March 2011*.

Anderson, A., Johnston, W., & McDonald, A. (2013). Information literacy in adult returner students. *Library and Information Review, 37*(114), 55–73.

Anderson, A., McDonald, A., & Johnston, W. (2011). Experiences of adult learners studying on the Pre-Entry Access course at the university of Strathclyde. In *Paper presented at the Annual conference of the Scottish Education Research Association, Stirling, Scotland, 24th November 2011*.

Anderson, A., & Soden, R. (2002). Peer interaction and argumentative reasoning. In R. Nata (Ed.), *Progress in education* (Vol. 7) (pp. 81–108). New York: Nova Science Publishers Inc.

Armstrong, C., Boden, D., Town, S., Wooley, M., Webber, S., & Abell, A. (2005). CILIP defines information literacy for the UK. *Library and Information Update, 4*, 22–25.

Association of College and Reseach Libraries. (2000). *Information Literacy Competence Standards for Higher Education*. Chicago: American Library Association.

Association of College and Research Libraries. (2015). *Framework for information literacy for higher education*. http://www.ala.org/acrl/standards/ilframework.

Attar, D. (2005). Dismay and disappointment: perspectives of inexperienced adult learners on becoming webpage readers. *International Journal of Educational Research, 43*, 495–508.

Badke, W. (2008). A rationale for information literacy as a credit-bearing discipline. *Journal of Information Literacy, 2*(1), 1–22. http://dx.doi.org/10.11645/2.1.42.

Barnett, R., & Coate, K. (2005). *Engaging the curriculum in higher education*. Maidenhead: Society for Research into Higher Education and Open University Press.

Baron, J. (1994). *Thinking and deciding*. Cambridge: Cambridge University Press.

Behar-Horensen, L. S., & Niu, L. (2011). Teaching critical thinking skills in higher education: a review of the literature. *Journal of College Teaching and Learning, 8*, 25–41.

Biggs, J. B. (1987). *Student approaches to learning and studying*. Melbourne: Australian Council for Educational Research.

Biggs, J. B. (2011). *Teaching for quality learning at university: What the student does*. Maidenhead: Open University Press.

Billig, M. (1987). *Arguing and thinking: A rhetorical approach to social psychology*. Cambridge, UK: Cambridge University Press.

Bloom, B. S. (1956). *Taxonomy of educational objectives: The cognitive domain*. New York: Donald MacKay.
Bloom, B. S. (1984). *Taxonomy of educational objectives: The classification of goals. Book 1: Cognitive domain*. New York: Longman.
Bravender, P., McClure, H., & Schaub, G. (2015). *Teaching information literacy threshold concepts: Lesson plans for librarians*. Chicago, IL: Association of College and Research Libraries.
Brem, S. K., Russell, J., & Weems, L. (2001). Science on the web: student evaluations of scientific arguments. *Discourse Processes, 32*, 191–213.
Brookfield, S. (1987). *Developing critical thinking*. Milton Keynes: SRHE and Open University Press.
Bruce, C. (2008). *Informed Learning*. Chicago: IL Association of College of Research Libraries.
Brunetti, K., Hofer, A. R., & Townsend, L. (2014). Interdisciplinarity and information literacy instruction: a threshold concepts approach. In C. O'Mahoney, A. Buchanan, M. O'Rourke, & B. Higgs (Eds.), *Threshold concepts: From personal practice to communities of practice, Proceedings of the National Academy's Sixth Annual conference and the Fourth Biennial Threshold Concepts conference* (pp. 89–93). Cork, Ireland: NAIRTL. http://www.nairtl.ie/documents/EPub_2012Proceedings.pdf#page=99.
Buckland, M. (1991). Information as thing. *Journal of the American Society for Information Science, 42*, 351–360.
Cole, M. (1996). *Cultural psychology: A once and future discipline*. Cambridge, MA: Harvard University Press.
Cottrell, S. (2003). *The study skills handbook* (3rd ed.). Basingstoke: Palgrave MacMillan.
Cranton, P. (2006). *Understanding and promoting transformative learning: A guide for educators of adults*. San Francisco: Jossey-Bass.
Crook, C. (1998). Children as computer users: the case of collaborative learning. *Computers and Education, 30*, 237–247.
Deuze, M. (2006). Participation, remediation, bricolage: considering principal components of a digital culture. *The Information Society, 22*, 63–75.
Doise, W., & Mugny, G. (1984). *The social development of the intellect*. Oxford: Pergamon.
Egan, M., & Shera, J. (1952). Foundations of a theory of bibliography. *Library Quarterly, 44*, 125–137.
Eisenberg, M. B., & Berkowitz, R. E. (1990). *Information problem solving: The Big Six Skills approach to library and information skills instruction*. Norwood: Ablex.
Elmborg, J. (2006). Critical information literacy: implications for instructional practice. *Journal of Academic Leadership, 32*, 192–199.
Ennis, R. H. (1987). A taxonomy of critical thinking dispositions and abilities. In J. B. Baron, & R. Sternberg (Eds.), *Teaching thinking skills: Theory and practice*. New York: W. H. Freeman and Co.
Entwistle, N. J. (2001). Styles of learning and approaches to studying in higher education. *Kybernetes, 30*, 593–602.
Entwistle, N. J. (2007). Research into student learning and university teaching. In N. Entwistle, & P. Tomlinson (Eds.), *Student learning and university teaching: British journal of educational psychology monograph series II* (Vol. 4) (pp. 1–18).
Entwistle, N. J., & Tomlinson, P. (2007). In *Student learning and university teaching: British journal of educational psychology monograph series II* (Vol. 4) (pp. 1–18).
Fallis, D. (2006). Social epistemology and information science. *Annual Review of Information Science and Technology, 40*, 475–519.
Flavell, J. H. (1976). Metacognitive aspects of problem solving. In L. B. Resnick (Ed.), *The nature of intelligence* (pp. 231–235). Hillsdale, NJ: Lawrence Erlbaum Associates.
Flavell, J. H. (1979). Metacognition and cognitive monitoring. *American Psychologist, 34*, 906–911.
Floridi, L. (2002). On defining library and information science as applied philosophy of information. *Social Epistemology, 16*, 37–49.
Freire, P. (2006). *Pedagogy of the oppressed*. New York: Continuum International Publishing Group.

Fry, H., Ketteridge, S., & Marshall, S. (2003). *A handbook for teaching and learning in higher education: Enhancing academic practice* (2nd ed.). London: Kogan Page.
Garrison, D. R., & Akyol, Z. (2015). Toward the development of a metacognition construct for communities of inquiry. *Internet and Higher Education, 24*, 66–71.
Gick, M. L., & Holyoak, K. J. (1980). Analogical problem solving. *Cognitive Psychology, 12*, 306–355.
Glaser, B. G. (1992). *Emergence vs forcing: Basics of grounded theory analysis*. Mill Valley, CA: The Sociology Press.
Halpern, D. F. (2007). The nature and nurture of critical thinking. In R. J. Sternberg, H. L. Roediger, III, & D. F. Halpern (Eds.), *Critical thinking in psychology*. Cambridge: Cambridge University Press.
Halverson, K. L., Siegel, M. A., & Freyermouth, S. K. (2010). Non-science majors' critical evaluation of websites in a biotechnology course. *Journal of Science Education and Technology, 19*, 612–620.
Hammer, D., & Elby, A. (2002). On the form of a personal epistemology. In B. K. Hofer, & P. R. Pintrich,. (Eds.), *Personal epistemology: The psychology of beliefs about knowledge and knowing*. Mahwah, NJ: Erlbaum.
Harris, B. R. (2008). Communities as necessary in information literacy development: challenging the standards. *Journal of Academic Librarianship, 34*, 248–255.
Harvey, L., Moon, S., Geall, V., & Bower, R. (1997). *Graduates' work: Organisational change and students' attributes*. Birmingham: Centre for Research into Quality and the Association of Graduate Recruiters, University of Central England.
Heinstrom, J. (2010). *From fear to flow: Personality and information interaction*. Oxford: Chandos.
Hepworth, M., & Walton, G. (2009). *Teaching information literacy for inquiry based learning*. Oxford: Chandos Publishing.
Hofer, B. K. (2001a). Dimensionality and disciplinary differences in personal epistemology. *Contemporary Educational Psychology, 25*, 378–405.
Hofer, B. K. (2001b). Personal epistemology research: implications for learning and teaching. *Journal of Educational Psychology Review, 13*, 353–383.
Hofer, B. K. (2004). Epistemological understanding as a metacognitive process: thinking aloud during online searching. *Educational Psychologist, 39*, 43–55.
Hofer, B. K., & Pintrich, P. R. (1997). The development of epistemological theories: beliefs about knowledge and knowing and their relation to learning. *Review of Educational Research, 67*, 88–140.
Hofer, B. K., & Sinatra, G. M. (2010). Epistemology, metacognition and self-regulation: musings from an emerging field. *Metacognition Learning, 5*, 113–120.
Hofer, A., Townsend, L., & Brunetti, K. (2012). Troublesome concepts and information literacy: investigating threshold concepts for IL instruction. *Portal: Libraries and the Academy, 12*(4), 387–405.
Horton, F. W. (2008). Understanding information literacy: a primer. In The Information Society Division, Communications and Information Sector (Ed.), *UNESCO information for all programme*. Paris: UNESCO.
Horton, F. W. (2011). Information literacy advocacy – Woody's ten commandments. *Library Trends, 60*(2, Fall 2011), 262–276.
Howe, C. J., Rodgers, C., & Tolmie, A. (1990). Physics in the primary school: peer interaction and the understanding of floating and sinking. *European Journal of Psychology of Education, 5*, 459–475.
Howe, C. J., Tolmie, A., Anderson, A., & Mackenzie, M. (1992). Conceptual knowledge in physics: the role of group interaction in computer-supported teaching. *Learning and Instruction, 2*, 161–183.
Howe, C. J., Tolmie, A., & Rodgers, C. (1992). The acquisition of conceptual knowledge in science by primary school children: group interaction and the understanding of motion down an incline. *British Journal of Developmental Psychology, 10*, 113–130.

Hutchins, E. (1995). *Cognition in the wild*. Cambridge, Mass: MIT Press.
Ingwersen, P. (1992). *Information retrieval interaction*. London: Taylor Graham.
Irzik, G. (2000). Back to basics: a philosophical critique of constructivism. *Science and Education, 9*, 621–639.
Jackson, P.A. (2007). Integrating information literacy into Blackboard: building campus partnerships for successful student learning. *Journal of Academic Librarianship, 33*(4), 454–461.
Jansen, B. J., Spink, A., & Saracevic, T. (2000). Real life, real users and real needs: a study and analysis of user queries on the web. *Information Processing and Management, 36*, 207–227.
Jerkov, A., Sofronijeic, A., Straniic, D. K., & from the University of Belgrade, University Library (2015). Smart and sustainable library: information literacy hub of a New City. In *Paper presented at the 3rd European conference on information literacy, Tallinn, Estonia, October 19–22, 2015*.
Johnston, W. (2010). *The first year at university: Teaching students in transition*. Society for Research into Higher Education and Open University Press.
Johnston, B., & Watson, A. (2004). Participation, reflection and integration for business and lifelong learning: pedagogical challenges of the integrative studies programme of the University of Strathclyde business school. *Journal of Workplace Learning, 16*, 53–62.
Johnston, B., & Watson, A. (2006). Employability: approaches to developing student career awareness and reflective practice in undergraduate business studies. In P. Tynjälä, J. Välimaa, & G. Boulton-Lewis (Eds.), *Higher education and working life*. Pergamon: EARLI.
Johnston, B., & Watson, A. (September 3, 2009). Key principles for developing graduates for the 21st century: lessons from a decade of practice and development in business education. *SEDA Journal: Educational Developments* (10), 21–24.
Johnston, B., & Webber, S. (1999). Information literacy as an academic discipline: an action research approach to developing a credit bearing class for business undergraduates. In M. Klasson, B. Lughridge, & S. Loof (Eds.), *New fields for research in the 21st century. Proceedings of the 3rd British Nordic conference on library and information studies; April 12–14, 1999, Boras, Sweden*. Boras: University College of Boras.
Johnston, B., & Webber, S. (2003). Information literacy in higher education: a review and case study. *Studies in Higher Education, 28*(3), 335–352.
Johnston, B., & Webber, S. (2006). As we may think: information literacy as a discipline for the information age. *Research Strategies, 20*(3), 108–121.
Jones, S., & Allen, J. (2012). Evaluating psychology library skills and experiences. *Psychology Teaching Review, 18*, 94–115.
Keen, A. (2015). *The internet is not the answer*. New York: Atlantic Books.
King, A. (1993). From sage of the stage to guide on the side. *College Teaching, 41*, 30–35.
King, P. M., & Kitchener, K. S. (1994). *Developing reflective judgment: Understanding and promoting intellectual growth and critical thinking in adolescents and adults*. San Francisco: Jossey-Bass.
Kitchenham, A. (2008). The evolution of John Mezirow's transformative learning theory. *Journal of Transformative Education, 6*, 104–123.
Kitcher, P. (1994). *The advancement of science: Science without legend, objectivity without illusions*. New York: Oxford University Press.
Konimos, N. (2014). *The age of intelligent cities*. New York, London: Routledge.
Ku, K. Y. L., & Ho, I. T. (2010). Metacognitive strategies that enhance critical thinking. *Metacognition Learning, 5*, 251–267.
Kuiper, E., Volman, M., & Teswel, J. (2009). Developing Web literacy in collaborative inquiry activities. *Computers and Education, 52*, 668–680.
Kuhn, D. (1991). *The skills of argument*. Cambridge: Cambridge University Press.
Kuhn, D. (2000). Metacognitive development. *Current Directions in Psychological Science, 9*, 178–181.
Kuhn, D., Cheney, R., & Weinstock, M. (2000). The development of epistemological understanding. *Cognitive Development, 15*, 309–328.

Kuhn, D., & Dean, D. (2004). Metacognition: a bridge between cognitive psychology and educational practice. *Theory into Practice, 43*, 268–273.

Kuhn, D., & Park, S.-H. (2005). Epistemological understanding and the development of intellectual values. *International Journal of Educational Research, 43*, 111–124.

Kuhn, D., Shaw, V., & Felton, M. (1997). Effects of dyadic interaction on argumentative reasoning. *Cognition and Instruction, 15*(3), 287–316.

Lai, E. (2011). *Critical thinking: A literature review*. Pearson Research Report. Available online at http://images.pearsonassessments.com/images/tmrs/CriticalThinkingReviewFINAL.pdf.

Lanier, J. (2013). *Who owns the future?* New York: Simon and Schuster.

Latour, B. (1987). *Science in action*. Cambridge, MA: Harvard University Press.

Latour, B., & Woolgar, S. (1986). *Laboratory life: The (social) construction of scientific facts*. Princeton: Princeton University Press.

Lazonder, A. W. (2000). Exploring novice users' training needs in searching information on the WWW. *Journal of Computer Assisted Learning, 16*, 326–335.

Lehman, D. R., & Nisbett, R. E. (1990). A longitudinal study of the effects of undergraduate training on reasoning. *Developmental Psychology, 26*, 952–960.

Limberg, L., Alexandersson, M., Lantz-Andersson, A., & Folkesson, L. (2008). What matters? Shaping meaningful learning through teaching information literacy. *Libri, 58*(2), 82–91.

Lindstrom, J., & Shonrick, D. D. (2006). Faculty-librarian collaboration to achieve integration of information literacy. *Reference and User Services Quarterly, 46*(1), 18–23.

Lloyd, A. (2010). *Information literacy landscapes*. Oxford: Chandos.

MacLellan, E., & Soden, R. (2008). Successful learners, confident individuals, responsible citizens and effective contributors to society: exploring the nature of learning and its implications in curriculum for excellence. *Scottish Educational Review, 40*, 29.

Marton, F., & Säljö, R. (1997). Approaches to learning. In F. Marton, D. J. Hounsell, & N. J. Entwistle (Eds.), *The experience of learning* (pp. 39–58). Edinburgh: Scottish Academic Press.

Mason, P. (2015). *PostCapitalism: A guide to our future*. London: Alan Lane.

McKeough, A., Lupart, J. L., & Marini, A. (2010). *Teaching for transfer: Fostering generalisation in learning*. New York: Routledge.

McPeck, J. E. (1981). *Critical thinking and education*. Oxford: Martin Robertson.

Meadows, S. (2006). *The child as thinker: The development and acquisition of cognition in childhood*. New York: Routledge.

Means, M. L., & Voss, J. F. (1996). Who reasons well? Two studies of informal reasoning among children of different grade, ability and knowledge levels. *Cognition and Instruction, 14*(2), 139–178.

Medaille, A., & Shannon, A. (2012). Co-teaching relationships among librarians and other information professionals. *Collaborative Librarianship, 4*(4), 132–148.

Merriam, S. B. (November 2004). The role of cognitive development in Mezirow's transformational learning theory. *Adult Education Quarterly, 55*(1), 60–68.

Meyer, D. L. (2009). The poverty of constructivism. *Educational Philosophy and Theory, 41*, 332–341.

Meyer, J. H. F., & Land, R. (2003). Threshold concepts and troublesome knowledge: linkages to ways of thinking and practising within the disciplines. In C. Rust (Ed.), *Improving student learning theory and practice – 10 years on* (pp. 412–424). Oxford Centre for Staff and Learning Development.

Meyer, J. H. F., & Land, R. (2005). Threshold concepts and troublesome knowledge (2): Epistemological considerations and a conceptual framework for teaching and learning. *Higher Education, 49*, 373–388.

Meyer, J. H. F., Land, R., & Baillie, C. (Eds.). (2010). *Threshold concepts and transformational learning*. Rotterdam: Sense Publishers.

Mezirow, J. (1978). Perspective transformation. *Adult Education, XXVIII*(2), 100–110.

Mezirow, J. (2000). *Learning as transformation: Critical perspectives on a theory in progress*. San Francisco: Jossey Bass.

Mezirow, J., & Taylor, E. W. (2009). *Transformative learning in practice: Insights from community, workplace and higher education*. San Francisco: Jossey-Bass.

Min, B. W. (2012). Next-generation library information service 'smart library'. *Environment, 9*, 11.

Moeller, S., Joseph, A., Lau, J., & Carbo, T. (2011). Towards media and information literacy indicators. In *Background document of the expert meeting, November 4–6, 2010, Bangkok, Thailand*. UNESCO. Paris 2011.

Morozov, E. (2015). Socialise the data centres. *New Left Review, 91*, 45–66.

Mounce, M. (2010). Working together: Academic librarians and faculty collaborating to improve students' information literacy skills: A literature review 2000–2009. *Reference Librarian, 51*(4), 300–320.

Mulnix, J. W. (2012). Thinking critically about critical thinking. *Educational Philosophy and Theory, 44*, 464–479.

Newman, M. (2012). Calling transformative learning into question: some mutinous thoughts. *Adult Education Quarterly, 62*, 36–55.

Newton, P., Driver, R., & Osborne, J. (1999). The place of argumentation in the pedagogy of school science. *International Journal of Science Education, 21*(5), 553–576.

Nicholas, D., Huntington, P., Williams, P., & Dobrowolski, T. (2006). The digital information consumer. In A. Spink, & C. Cole (Eds.), *New directions in information behavior*. Dordrecht: Springer.

Nisbett, R. E., Fong, G. T., Lehman, D. R., & Cheng, P. W. (1987). Teaching reasoning. *Science, 238*, 625–631.

Norman, D. (2013). *The psychology of everyday things*. New York: Basic Books.

Oakleaf, M. (2014). A roadmap for assessing student learning using the new framework for information literacy for higher education. *Journal of Academic Librarianship, 40*, 510–514.

O'Donnell, V., & Tobell, J. (2007). The transition of adult students to higher education: legitimate peripheral participation in a community of practice? *Adult Education Quarterly, 57*, 312–328.

Osborne, J. (2014). *Constructivism: Critiques. Encyclopedia of science education*. Dordrecht: Springer.

Palincsar, A. S. (1998). Social constructivist perspectives on teaching and learning. *Annual Review of Psychology, 49*, 345–375.

Pappacharissi, Z. (2002). The virtual sphere: the internet as a public sphere. *New Media and Society, 4*, 9–27.

Perkins, D. N. (1985). Postprimary education has little impact on informal reasoning. *Journal of Educational Psychology*, 77, 562–571.

Perkins, D. N. (1989). Reasoning as it is and as it could be: an empirical perspective. In D. M. Topping, D. C. Crowell, & V. N. Kobayashi (Eds.), *Thinking across cultures: The third international conference on thinking* (pp. 175–194). Hillsdale, NJ: Erlbaum.

Perkins, D. N., Allen, R., & Hafner, J. (1983). Difficulties in everyday reasoning. In J. Maxwell (Ed.), *Thinking: An interdisciplinary report*.

Perry, W. G. (1970). *Forms of intellectual and ethical development in the college years: A scheme*. San Francisco: Jossey-Bass.

Pilerot, O., & Lindberg, J. (2011). The concept of information literacy in policy-making texts: an imperialistic project? *Library Trends, 60*(2, Fall 2011), 238–260.

Prensky, M. (2001). Digital natives, digital immigrants, Part1. *On the Horizon, 9*, 1–6.

Pritchard, P. A. (2010). The embedded science librarian: Partner in curriculum design and delivery. *Journal of Library Administration, 50*(4), 373–379.

Reason, J. (1990). *Human error*. Cambridge: Cambridge University Press.

Resnick, L. B., & Nelson-LeGall, S. (1997). Socialising intelligence. In L. Smith, J. Dockrell, & P. Tomlinson (Eds.), *Piaget, Vygotsky, and beyond* (pp. 145–158). London: Routledge.

Robinson, F. P. (1978). *Effective study* (6th ed.). New York: Harper & Row.

Rogoff, B. (1998). Cognition as a collaborative process. In W. Damon, D. Kuhn, & R. Siegler (Eds.), *Handbook of child psychology: Vol. 2. Cognition, language, and perception* (5th ed.) (pp. 679–744). New York: Wiley.

Rosling, A., & Littlemore, K. (2011). Improving Student Mental Models in a New University Information Setting. In R. Rikowski (Ed.), *Digitization Perspectives* (pp. 89–101).

Schommer, M. (1990). Effects of beliefs about the nature of knowledge on comprehension. *Journal of Educational Psychology*, 498–504.

Schwartz, B. B., Neuman, Y., Gil, J., & Ilya, M. (2003). Construction of collective and individual knowledge in argumentative activity. *The Journal of the Learning Sciences, 12*(2), 219–256.

Scriven, M., & Paul, R. (2008). *Our concept for critical thinking. Foundation for critical thinking.* Available at http://www.criticalthinking.org/aboutCT/ourConceptCT.cfm.

Secker, J., & Coonan, E. (2013). In J. Secker, & E. Coonan (Eds.), *Rethinking information literacy: A practical framework for supporting learning*. London: Facet Publishing.

Shera, J. (1961). Social epistemology, general semantics and librarianship. *Wilson Library Bulletin, 35*, 767–770.

Shera, J. (1965). *Libraries and the organisation of knowledge*. London: Crosby and Lockwood.

Shera, J. (1970). *Sociological foundations of librarianship*. New York: Asia Publishing House.

Strauss, A. L., & Corbin, J. (1990). *Basics of qualitative research: Grounded theory procedures and techniques*. London: Sage.

Tanner, K. D. (2012). Promoting student metacognition. *CBE-Life Sciences Education, 11*, 113–120.

Ten Dam, G., & Volman, M. (2004). Critical thinking as a citizenship competence: teaching strategies. *Learning and Instruction, 14*, 359–379.

Thomas, I. (2009). Critical thinking, transformative learning, sustainable education, and problem-based learning in universities. *Journal of Transformative Education*, 7, 245–264.

Tisdell, E. J. (2008). Critical media literacy and transformative learning: drawing on pop culture and entertainment media in teaching for diversity in adult higher education. *Journal of Transformative Education, 6*, 48–67.

Townsend, L. (2014). Interdisciplinarity and information literacy Instruction: a threshold concepts approach. In C. O'Mahoney, A. Buchanan, M. O'Rourke, & B. Higgs (Eds.), *Threshold concepts: From personal practice to communities of practice, Proceedings of the National Academy's Sixth Annual conference and the Fourth Biennial Threshold Concepts conference* (pp. 89–93). Cork, Ireland: NAIRTL. http://www.nairtl.ie/documents/EPub_2012Proceedings.pdf#page=99.

UNESCO. (2003). *The Prague declaration – Towards an information literate society*. Available http://portal.unesco.org/ci/en/ev.php-URL_ID=19636&URL_DO=DO_PRINTPAGE&URL_SECTION=201.html. Accessed 06.06.11.

UNESCO. (2005). *The Alexandria proclamation on information literacy and lifelong learning*. Available http://www.ifla.org/III/wsis/BeaconInfSoc.html. Accessed 06.06.11.

UNESCO. (2006). *High-level Colloquium on information literacy and lifelong learning*. Available http://www.ifla.org/III/wsis/High-Level-Colloquium.pdf. Accessed 06.06.11.

UNESCO. (2015). *Keystones to foster inclusive knowledge societies: Access to information and knowledge, freedom of expression, privacy, and ethics on a global internet. Paris, UNESCO. "Final Study".*

Vermunt, J. D. (2007). The power of teaching-learning environments to influence student learning. In N. Entwistle, & P. Tomlinson (Eds.), *Student learning and university teaching: BJEP monograph series II* (Vol. 4) (pp. 73–90). London: British Psychological Society.

Von Glasersfeld, E. (1995). *Radical constructivism: A way of knowing and learning. Studies in Mathematics education series: 6*. Bristol: Falmer Press.

Vygotsky, L. S. (1978). *Mind in society: The development of higher psychological processes.* Cambridge, Mass: Harvard University Press.

Walton, G., & Hepworth, M. (2011). A longitudinal study of changes in learner's cognitive states during and following and information literacy teaching intervention. *Journal of Documentation, 67*(3), 449–479.

Webber, S., & Johnston, B. (2000). Conceptions of information literacy: new perspectives and implications. *Journal of Information Science, 26*(6), 381–397.

Webber, S., Boon, S., & Johnston, B. (2005). A comparison of UK academics' conceptions of information literacy in two disciplines: English and Marketing. *Library and Information Research, 29*(93), 4–15.

Whitmire, E. (2003). Epistemological beliefs and the information-seeking behavior of undergraduates. *Library and Information Science Research, 25*, 127–142.

Willingham, D. T. (2007). Critical thinking: why is it so hard to teach? *American Educator, Summer*, 8–19.

Wilson, C., Carolyn, Grizzle, Alton, Tuazon, Ramon, et al. (2011). *Media and information literacy curriculum for teachers*. Paris: UNESCO.

Wood, D., Bruner, J. S., & Ross, G. (1976). The role of tutoring in problem solving. *Journal of Child Psychology and Psychiatry, 17*(2), 89–100.

INDEX

'*Note:* Page numbers followed by "b" indicate boxes.'

A

Access course, 19–20, 22–23, 26, 28
ACRL (2000) Standards, 103
  pedagogical attraction for ACRL, 104
  pedagogical changes, 106–107
ACRL (2015) Revised Framework, 103
  framework logic, 105
  information literacy in, 113–114
  pedagogical attraction for ACRL, 104
  pedagogical changes, 106–107
  pedagogical implications, 112–113
  threshold concepts, 107–108
    ACRL Framework, 109–110
    authority, 110
    Delphi study, 108
    information creation, 110
    information value, 110–111
    initial conclusions, 111–112
    research as inquiry, 111
    scholarship as conversation, 111
    searching as strategic exploration, 111
Activity perspective, 45–46
Adult returner students, information literacy in, 19
  background context, 19
    access course, 20
    additional learning tasks, 21–22
    mature students, 20
    pre-entry course, 20–21
  corroborative studies, 29–31
  study itself, 22
    information literacy, 23–25
    'participants' perceptions of information use, 22–23
    patterns of learning, 25–27
    transformational learning, 27–29
Affordances, 3–4
Alexandra Proclamation, 119
Argumentative reasoning, 40
  number of abilities, 41
  quality, 41–42
    bleak picture, 44
    domain-generality *vs.* specificity issue, 46
    information literacy activities, 47
    'issue of participants' motivation, 44–45
    makes-sense epistemology, 43
    theoretical set of issues, 45–46
    unimpressive argumentative reasoning performances, 43–44
    vexed personal decision, 44
    written task, 42–43
  skills, 50
Authority, 110

B

Belief/theory approach, 58
Beliefs, 57–58

C

Capitalism, 140
'Childrens' performance, 61
Collaborators, 49–50
Comprehension, 12
Conceptual conflict, 68–70
Constructivism, 67, 146–148
  constructivist pedagogy in practice, 71b–72b
  critique of, 73
  intuitive physics, 69b–70b
  learners, 68
  pedagogy, 70
  sources, 68–70
  theory of, 67–68
Constructivist pedagogy, 140, 147
  in practice, 71b–72b

Corroborative studies, 29–31
Critical thinking, 12, 37, 41, 53–54. *See also* Epistemological thinking
 advertisements and political manifestos, 40
 components, 40
 elements, 38–39
 information-seeking process, 39–40
 key components, 38
 overall definition, 39
 pedagogical implications, 38
 pedagogy and, 47–48
  argumentative reasoning skills, 50
  collaborators, 49–50
  instructional approaches, 48
  library/digital-skills-based notion, 50–51
  meta-analytic review, 48–49
  qualitative review, 49
  sequence of sessions, 52
  seven-session MOOC, 51–52
  'short-course' approach, 51
Cultural tools, 13
Curriculum
 development, 93–95
  curriculum inquiry and development, 83
  information literacy and, 95–96
  psychological literature, 84
 inquiry and practice, 92–93

D

Deep approaches, 74–75
'Deep' learning, 74–75
'Deep' processing strategies, 26
Developmental approach, 58
Developmental psychology, 12
Digital culture, 4–5
Digital information, 5
Digital literacy, 5
Digital participation
 benefits, 8–9
 in information culture, 6
  aspects, 7
  awareness, 7
  information literacy, 8
  technological entity, 8

E

ECIL conferences. *See* European Conference on Information Literacy conferences (ECIL conferences)
Epistemic metacognition, 65–66
Epistemological development, 106
Epistemological thinking, 53. *See also* Critical thinking
 absolutist level of development, 54–56
 beliefs, 57–58
 complications, 58–59
 development, 54–56
 developmental and belief/theory approach, 58
 fundamental epistemological assumptions, 58
 knowledge and theory, 56–57
 predictable developmental progression, 59–60
 strategy use and cognitive processing, 59
 teaching and learning experiences, 59
 theoretical approaches, 57
 in undergraduate students, 56
Ethics, 125–126
European Conference on Information Literacy conferences (ECIL conferences), 8–9
Evaluating, 54–56, 60, 62–65

F

Fairly rudimentary study techniques, 26
Freedom of expression, 125

G

Global Alliance for Partnerships on Media and Information Literacy (GAPMIL), 121, 126

H

Halpern's Critical Thinking Assessment Test, 64–65
Horton, Forest Woody, 118–121

I

IFLA. *See* International Federation of Library Associations (IFLA)
IL. *See* Information literacy (IL)

Information, 3–4, 6
  behaviour, 9
  creation, 110
  ecosystems, 4
  information-seeking process, 39–40
  society, 3
  value, 110–111
Information culture, 3–5
  affordances, 3–4
  digital information, 5
  digital participation, 6
    aspects, 7
    awareness, 7
    information literacy, 8
    technological entity, 8
  familiar aspects, 9
    information behaviour, 9
    key issue, 10
    perspectives, 11
    sociocultural dimension, 9–10
    'wise and ethical' use of information, 10
  information literacy, 6, 8–9
  information society, 3
  learning and use of cultural tools, 4
  psychology and psychological insights, 11–13
Information literacy (IL), 6, 8–9, 23, 67, 83, 103, 115, 131. *See also* Transformational learning
  and curriculum development, 95–96
  deciding on trustworthiness of sources, 24–25
  familiar aspects, 9
  finding and using sources, 23
  information behaviour, 9
  key issue, 10
  New Curriculum for, 96
  perspectives, 11
  primer, 118–121
  sociocultural dimension, 9–10
  teaching
    within lifelong learning contexts, 150–151
    within universities, 148–150
  'wise and ethical' use of information, 10
Information Literacy Lifecycle, 119
Inquiry, research as, 111
Instructional approaches, 48
International Federation of Library Associations (IFLA), 121
Internet Age, social epistemology in, 136
  economic information, 137
  growth of Internet, 138
  social and economic reality, 141
  technological businesses, 139
  UNESCO, 139
Internet Universality, 124
Intuitive physics, 69b–70b

K

Knowledge Societies Final Study, 124
  keystone fields, 125
  MIL in Knowledge Societies, 126–127

L

'Lay' theory of teaching and learning, 67
Learning, 12, 67, 71b–72b. *See also* Transformational learning
  process, 67–68
  surface approaches to, 74–75
  unguided discovery, 73
'Learning through doing' approach, 26
Librarianship, 141
  Austerity politics, 142
  organisational development, 143
  smart libraries for smart cities, 144–145

M

Makes-sense epistemology, 43
Management Development Programme (MDP), 148
Mature students, 20
MDP. *See* Management Development Programme (MDP)
Meaning schemes, 91
Media and information literacy (MIL), 121–124
  in Knowledge Societies, 126–127
Metacognition, 48, 60. *See also* Epistemic metacognition
  aspects, 62–63
  beneficial effects of structured peer interaction, 62
  'childrens' performance, 61
  confusion, 62–63
  developmental change, 60–61

Metacognition (*Continued*)
possibilities for learning, 63
proceedings, 64
searching database for information, 65
Tanner's three areas for, 63
think-aloud protocols, 64–65
MIL. *See* Media and information literacy (MIL)
Mind maps, 74
Monitoring, 60, 62–65
MOOC, 51–52
Multiplist epistemology, 54–56
Myside bias, 42–43

N

New Curriculum for information literacy, 96
appendices, 99–100
commentary, 100–101
curriculum
aim, 96–97
attributes, 97–98
implementation, 99
uses, 98–99
Secker and Coonan's, 83–84
Newtonian theory, 69b–70b

O

'One-shot slot' approach, 50–51
'One-shot' teaching interventions, 50
One-slot-shot scenario, 112–113
Online access, 125
Organisational commitment, 149

P

Patterns of learning, 25. *See also* Transformational learning
academic disciplines, 26
'deep' processing strategies, 26
fairly rudimentary study techniques, 26–27
study-related matters, 26
Pedagogical/pedagogy, 70, 84, 89, 92
argumentative reasoning skills, 50
changes, 106–107
collaborators, 49–50
and critical thinking, 47–48
implications, 112–113
instructional approaches, 48
library/digital-skills-based notion, 50–51
meta-analytic review, 48–49
qualitative review, 49
sequence of sessions, 52
seven-session MOOC, 51–52
'short-course' approach, 51
strategies, 3
Peer interaction, 70, 71b–72b
discrepancy of views, 68–70
Personality, 12
Perspective
change, 91
transformation, 85–86, 92
Piaget's theory, 68–70
Planning, 60, 62–65
Practice, 38–39, 45–46, 50
Pre-entry course, 20–21
Prior conceptions, 68, 69b–70b
Privacy, 125
Problem-solving, 11–12
Proclamations, 117–118
Pseudoevidence, 41–42
Psychological competencies, 3
Psychological tools, 13

R

R-O-A-M principles. *See* Rights, openness, accessibility and multistakeholder principles (R-O-A-M principles)
Relational human information behaviour, 4
Research as inquiry, 111
Resources, 57–58
Rights, openness, accessibility and multi-stakeholder principles (R-O-A-M principles), 124

S

SBS. *See* Strathclyde Business School (SBS)
Scholarship as conversation, 111
Scottish Bachelor-level degree, 19
Shared metacognition, 60
'Short-course' approach, 51
Skill, 45–46
Smart libraries for smart cities, 144–145
Smartphones, 8
Social epistemology, 3–5, 132
classical and revolutionary, 134
electronic resources, 135

Internet, 133
in Internet Age, 136
economic information, 137
growth of Internet, 138
social and economic reality, 141
technological businesses, 139
UNESCO, 139
and librarianship, 141
Austerity politics, 142
organisational development, 143
smart libraries for smart cities, 144–145
'old Encyclopaedia' problem, 135
pedagogy for, 145
constructivism, 146–148
information literacy teaching, 150–151
information literacy teaching within universities, 148–150
Social metacognition, 60
Social psychology, 12
Sound hypothesis, 61
SQ3R. *See* Survey, question, read, recall and review (SQ3R)
Strathclyde Business School (SBS), 148
Study skills, 19–21, 26, 74–75
Surface approaches to learning, 74–75
Survey, question, read, recall and review (SQ3R), 74

T

Tablet computers, 8
Teaching intervention, 44–45, 47–50
Technological entity, 8
Think-aloud protocols, 64–65
Threshold concepts, 107–108
ACRL Framework, 109–110
authority, 110
Delphi study, 108
information creation, 110
information value, 110–111
initial conclusions, 111–112
research as inquiry, 111
scholarship as conversation, 111
searching as strategic exploration, 111
Transactional human information behaviour, 4
Transformational learning, 27, 85. *See also* Patterns of learning
curriculum inquiry, 89
emancipation, 85–86
'fact-based' subjects, 90–91
information literacy, 90–91
interviewees, 27–28
metacognitive awareness of learning, 29
Newman's scepticism, 87
presuppositions, 28
retrospective claims, 88–89
theory of transformative learning, 86
Transmission view of learning, 67

U

UCAS. *See* Universities and Colleges Admissions System (UCAS)
UNESCO, 139
contributions
education, information, human rights and social justice, 115–117
information literacy primer, 118–121
MIL, 121–124
proclamations, 117–118
Knowledge Societies Final Study, 124
keystone fields, 125
MIL in Knowledge Societies, 126–127
Universities and Colleges Admissions System (UCAS), 20–21

V

Vexed personal decision, 44

W

'Well-formed' problems, 12–13
Wikipedia, 140
World Wide Web (WWW), 117

Y

Yale undergraduates, 31

Z

Zone of Proximal Development (ZPD), 44–45

FSC
www.fsc.org
MIX
Papier | Fördert gute Waldnutzung
FSC® C083411

Kolibri 360 GmbH
Ferdinand-Jühlke-Straße 7
99095 Erfurt, Deutschland
produktsicherheit@kolibri360.de